THE ULTIMATE GOLF INSTRUCTION GUIDE:

KEY TECHNIQUES FOR BECOMING A ZERO HANDICAP GOLFER OR BETTER

DR. PATRICK LEONARDI

SILVER EDUCATIONAL PUBLISHING

ARIZONA

Silver Educational Publishing
Published by Silver 8 Production LLC

Library of Congress Catalog Number: 2004097419
ISBN: 1-933023-09-0

Printed in the United States of America.

All photos by Melissa Heilman

MESSAGE FROM THE AUTHOR

Please maintain an open mind when reading this book. The techniques in this book are sometimes contradictory to what is conventionally taught. Sometimes past ways of doing or perceiving things are now extinct today. For example, over 500 years ago most people thought the world was flat. Of course, this is a myth and now everyone recognizes the truth that the world is round.

It was normal for professional baseball players to not wear helmets during a greater portion of the 20th century. Today if a batter didn't wear a helmet, he would be viewed as foolish and abnormal. Just like there are many ways to make a reliable car or quality house, there is more than one way to become skillful at golf. My techniques have made me improve at a much faster pace than any other techniques I have tried. It is possible that what I discovered could do the same for you. When I first started playing golf, my first score was 127. I now consistently shoot in the 60s, and I didn't even start playing at a very young age. Please keep in account that I'm not saying this to brag about my achievements. I just wanted to use myself as an example to show how my techniques can help you also. With practice and time, you also can reach your potential as a golfer.

What I teach can make the challenge of becoming more skillful at golf an easier journey. Based on my extensive knowledge of anatomy, I discovered my techniques through many years of trial and error. My mission is to share with you how my techniques may benefit your game. I want you to reach your potential and in the process make golf much more enjoyable. I want to make a difference. All the best. Dr. Patrick Leonardi

CONTENTS

Chapter 1
Reaching Your Potential

Golf is a great game; however, it is more fun when you play it well. In this book, there are techniques that can fulfill your potential as a golfer and make golf more fun. Golf is a lot easier than many coaches, professional players and amateurs make it out to be. In actuality, you are hitting a ball that doesn't move. All you have to do is hit the sweet spot of the club with the ball to get the best contact. In this way, the ball can be hit a certain distance time after time. Of course, it takes some practice, but proper technique will make it much easier to reach your goals faster. The techniques in this book are in some ways contradictory to what is out there on the market. This book is here to excel you through your golfing experience. Whether you see golf for yourself as a hobby, a passion, or professional career, this book should help you. This book is not only about trusting your swing but applying what you learn in an easy manner to hit the ball longer and more consistently at any target you choose to aim at. After learning these techniques and applying them with practice, you won't have to consciously say, "trust your swing." How many of us have gone up to the first tee with thoughts of self-doubt and fear of embarrassment? With these techniques, your self-doubt will reduce and your fear of embarrassment will subside. First off, begin to think big. If you never broke 100 before, you should not perceive 90 as unrealistic. Of course, there are certain stepping stones to take. Before making 90 your goal, make 95 your goal first. Once you reach 95, make 90 your goal next. Little steps with persistence will lead to your goals. However, in the back of your mind, don't think shooting even par or better is ever out of the picture in your life. If no one believes in you, believe in yourself. Your opinion of yourself ultimately will have the most lasting effect on your scores. Also, let go of your golf ego. Stop letting your self-worth be dependent on how good your next shot will be. Value yourself not on how talented you are at something but on how you treat others and the type of person you are. I know this is hard to do in this day and age of achievement. It seems in the media such as television, people are only valued if their talented, have lots of money and are the best at every possible endeavor. No wonder why many people are so stressed out! Begin to think different, and your game will be different. If you hit a great shot and get an eagle on a par 5, you should feel good but don't feel more worthy as a person because of this. However, if you hit a bad shot and miss the fairway on a drive, don't put yourself down and feel unworthy. In other words, separate your golf game from your self-worth. Your golf game will get better because this will put a lot less pressure on you when your about to hit a shot. This will also put golf in the prospective of something as fun and not a pressure-intense, competitive event that many people may want it to be.

It's good to compete but only compete against yourself. Whether you're in a golf tournament, a friendly game or just out there by yourself playing, learn to just do your individual best. Forget about the rest, including the stupid, half-complements from others like "that drive was much better than your last one." Sometimes it's better not to say anything. Start caring more about what is going through your mind and not what other people might be thinking about you especially when you're about to hit a golf shot. Who cares if you miss a 3-foot putt, or hit a drive into the trees? Don't feel embarrassed, it has happened to everyone who have played golf. With these techniques, however, these mishaps should decrease significantly and your scores will get better. The essentials of the golf swing are easy to learn. Learning this technique will lead to more consistent ball flight and predictability. Yes, it is true; golf can be predictable and consistent. A person can control what he or she chooses to score.

Chapter 2

The Essentials of the Zero Handicap or Better Golf Swing

The stance serves as the foundation of what will happen next. The feet should be about shoulders width apart. The front foot should be slightly open (*Figure 2.1a*) (*Figure 2.1b*).

Figure 2.1a. (For right-handed golfers) Observe how the front foot is slightly open and how the front shoulder is positioned higher than the left in the stance.

Figure 2.1b. (For left-handed golfers)

The weight distribution should be about 75% on the back foot and 25% on the front foot. Also, the back shoulder should be lower than the front shoulder when setting up to the ball. However, do not get too caught up in the weight distribution because simply taking your club back in the backswing will bring your weight back. Just make sure that most of your weight is not on your front foot at address. The interlocking grip works best with this technique. For right-handed golfers look at *Figure 2.2a, Figure 2.2b, Figure 2.2c*. For left-handed golfers look at *Figure 2.2d, Figure 2.2e, Figure 2.2f*. Copy my hand position on the grip exactly.

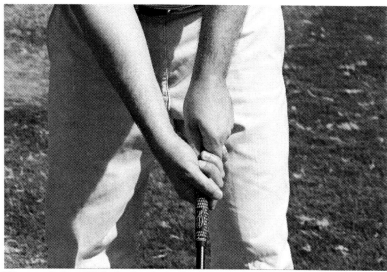

Figure 2.2a. This is the interlocking grip for right-handed golfers.

Figure 2.2b. This is the front view of the appropriate interlocking grip for the right-handed golfer.

Figure 2.2c. This is the interlocking grip for right-handed golfers photographed from behind.

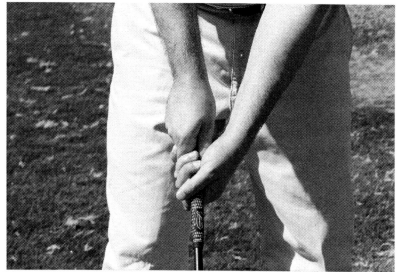

Figure 2.2d. This picture shows the interlocking grip for left-handed golfers.

Figure 2.2e. This is the front view of the appropriate interlocking grip for the left-handed golfer.

Figure 2.2f. This is the interlocking grip for left-handed golfers photographed from behind.

The backswing will start when you bring your hands back. As you bring your hands back, start bending your forward arm at the elbow. This is the left arm in right-handed golfers and the right arm in left-handed golfers. At the top of the backswing, the arm is bent at the elbow at approximately 90-95 degrees *(Figure 2.3a) (Figure 2.3b)*.

Figure: 2.3a. (For right-handed golfers) Bending at the elbow in the backswing will give you more power and control. Also, observe how the shaft never goes to parallel. In fact, this photo is taken at the end of the backswing.

Figure 2.3b. (For left-handed golfers).

This is the key position of the entire golf swing. Notice how baseball hitters bend their forward arms at the elbows during the backswing. Maximum power in golf is attained through bending this forward arm at the top of the backswing. Also, bending this arm will shorten your backswing. By doing this, the shaft of the golf club will not be going to parallel or past parallel in the backswing as in the standard golf swing. When a club goes parallel in the golf swing, this refers to the golf shaft in relation to the floor. Bending your forward elbow in the backswing will make the route to the ball much shorter and thus, create more accuracy in all golf shots and increase power. Most golfers have trouble hitting fairways on a very consistent basis with a driver due to the fact of a straight forward arm at the top of the backswing. Why do you think many golfers hit a 3-wood or an iron in place of a driver on many holes? This is because most of them may find it difficult to hit the fairway more than 50% of the time using a driver. Their percentage of hitting the fairway increases by using higher lofted clubs such as 3-woods and 5-woods. If professional golfers were limited to only hitting drivers off all par fours and par fives, the statistic of percentage of fairways hit would be far lower.

Hitting an iron in place of a driver off a par 4 or 5 is not what I call fun golf. Almost everyone loves to hit the ball far. There is no need to sacrifice power. In fact, hitting iron instead of driver will increase the length of the course and lead to higher scores. During the downswing, the weight is shifted from the back foot to the front foot. When the club hits the ball, your weight should be mostly on your front foot (85% front foot, 15% back foot) (*Figure 2.4a*) (*Figure 2.4b*).

Figure 2.4a. (For right-handed golfers)

The clubface just hit the ball. Observe how most

of the weight is on the front foot.

Figure 2.4b. (For left-handed golfers)

Your aim is to hit the ball on the center of the clubface. At the end of the follow-through (end of the swing) with driver, finish high to the sky. This means point the shaft of the club straight toward the sky and put the club to the side *(Figure 2.5a) (Figure 2.5b)*.

16

Figure 2.5a. (For right-handed golfers) Notice also the stiff forward leg. This is an indication that an excellent weight shift has just taken place.

Figure 2.5b. (For left-handed golfers)

This is done with only the following clubs: Driver, 3-wood, 4-wood, 5-wood, 3-iron, 4-iron and 5-iron. However, using clubs 6-iron, 7-iron, 8-

iron, 9-iron, pitching wedge and sand wedge just point the shaft of the club straight to the sky without putting the club to the side *(Figure 2.6a) (Figure 2.6b)*. If you are a right-handed golfer, extend your right arm directly overhead when doing this. Copy the arm position on this page.

Figure 2.6a. (For right-handed golfers)

Figure 2.6b. (For left-handed golfers)

The power of the golf swing using these essentials starts off with the feet. This power force is then transmitted to the legs during the start of the backswing. As the club starts to come down in the downswing, the upper legs transmit its power force to the hips and abdominal muscles. Right when the club is about to strike the ball, the triceps and shoulders now have this power force. Finally, this power force is transmitted from the triceps to the forearms and then to the wrists. The forward wrist is what propels the club forward. The back wrist is the guide; it stabilizes the clubface. An important essential of the zero handicap or better golf swing is always having the ball in the same position with every club. Look at *Figure 2.7a* and *Figure 2.7b.*

Figure 2.7a. (For right-handed golfers). The ball is at the same position at the level of the inside forward foot.

Figure 2.7b. (For left-handed golfers)

Specifically, the ball is in the same position at the level of the inside forward foot with every club. This is a very important essential. There is only one time the ball will not be in this position. This is when you need to hit a ball low (i.e., under a tree as in a knockdown shot). In only this case, the ball will be in the back of your stance between the back foot and middle of the stance. However, with this technique, this should not happen often because you will be in the fairway more often then you think.

The ball flight should correct on its own using this technique. If you are right-handed and hit the ball slightly left of the target, it may start to fade back into the target. If you are left-handed, it may draw into the target. If you are right-handed and hit the ball right of the target, it may draw into the target. If you are left-handed, it may fade back into the target. However, you must use these essentials of golf correctly to get this ball flight. If you are hitting the ball too low with your driver, add a little loft to the driver by raising the clubface slightly upward *(Figure 2.8a) (Figure 2.8b).* Believe me; this should increase your driving distance with driver. This will increase the angle of your ball flight.

Figure 2.8a. The clubface is placed with its normal loft at set-up.

Figure 2.8b. The clubface is angled slightly upward to increase loft.

Here are the essentials of the zero handicap or better golf swing. Study them, use every one them, and you should improve at a much faster pace.

Essentials of the Zero Handicap or Better Golf Swing

1. Feet are shoulders width apart at address with the back shoulder lower than the front shoulder.

2. The interlocking grip is used.

3. The ball is in the same position at the level of the inside forward foot with every club.

4. Forward arm is bent at the elbow at 90-95 degrees at top of the backswing (Key Position).

5. Weight begins to shift from the back foot to the forward foot when beginning the start of the downswing to hit the ball.

6. After the club hits the ball, you start to finish the downswing with a straight, stiff forward leg.

7. Finish high with the shaft pointed directly overhead toward the sky with clubs 6-iron, 7-iron, 8-iron, 9-iron, pitching wedge and sand wedge. The right arm (for right-handed golfers) is fully extended. The left arm is slightly bent at the elbow. When doing this essential, you should only think

about completely extending your right arm overhead at the end of the follow-through. Thus, the left arm will be in the correct position without thinking about it.

8. Finish high with the shaft pointed directly overhead toward the sky and put the club to the side with clubs driver, 3-wood, 4-wood, 5-wood, 3-iron, 4-iron and 5-iron.

Use these essentials and start having more fun playing golf. Do not be afraid to use the driver. The only way you can get better with driver is by using it. You will never get better with the driver by consistently using fairway woods and irons off the tee. Nothing quite feels like a well-struck drive that goes right at your intended target. Use your driver as often as possible on par fours and par fives. Your driver is not the hardest club to control. Like the putter, it takes practice and some patience. Every club in the golf bag should be equally easy to hit. Start perceiving the putter just as easy to hit as the driver. One reason why many golfers have trouble hitting the driver is that they do not use it enough in a golf round. This may have to do with certain philosophies of some golf instructors. When I first started to play golf, I went for a couple of golf lessons. This golf instructor (let us call him Mr. Instructor) used a camera to film me, which first made me feel he knew what he was doing. Mr. Instructor wanted to set me up the way he knew how to score a 78. Since 78 was his best score, he thought he knew best. Wow, getting a lesson from someone who could break 80, I was real fortunate. Well, not really! First off, he told me to first master the short irons before even thinking to hit the driver. It did not matter that I had a lot of power and could only help my game. He wanted me to keep hitting 8-irons until I could hit them straight. He said arrogantly, as if only he knew what was best, "you're not even ready to hit the driver." It was not because he ever saw me hit my driver; it was because I told him I was a beginning golfer. In his tunnel-vision mind, he believed no beginner should use the driver since traditional wisdom tells us the driver is so hard to hit. This to me is nonsense. The driver is not any harder to hit than the 3-wood or even 5-wood. It is all about perception. The common theory is that the driver is harder to hit because it is the longest club in the golf bag. The real reasons are that golfers don't use their drivers enough, and they are using less effective techniques. Many golfers are guilty of this. Perceive all your clubs as having equal skill to use, and with practice, you can have consistent and equal performance from each club.

Chapter 3
Course Management

Course management can be described as how one chooses to play a specific golf course. For example, choosing to hit a driver instead of a 3-wood is one example of course management. Use driver as much as possible. According to the USGA (United States Golf Association)[1], every 220 yards makes a golf course play harder by one stroke for the scratch golfer or zero handicap golfer. For many golfers, adding 220 yards plays about an extra stroke. So if you opt to hit a 3-wood off the tee instead of a driver, you essentially are making the course play longer. Using a 3-wood off the tee can equate to 25-30 yardage loss on a hole. This is because most golfers can hit a driver 25-30 yards further than the 3-wood. If you used 3-wood on 14 driving holes, this could amount to as much as 420 yards of additional yardage that is added to the course. This result is achieved by multiplying 14 holes x 30 yardages = 420 yards. If you divide 420 yards by 220 yards, the result is 1.9. This would make the course play 1.9 strokes harder if you are a scratch golfer or even harder if you have a handicap of one or greater. Remember a scratch golfer is defined as someone who is a zero handicap. In addition, the ideal scratch golfer hits average drives of 250 yards according to the USGA.

If one was to add 1.9 strokes to the course rating, a 71.8 course rating would now be a 73.7 course rating. There are two reasons why one should hit a 3-wood off the tee of a par 4 or par 5. The first reason is that a par 4 is reachable with a 3-wood. The second reason is that there is a water hazard

25

in the middle of the fairway in the approximate area of how far you hit your driver. Ignore the golfer you see who hits 2-irons or 3-irons off the tee of a par 4 or 5. Believe it or not, many of these players may find it hard to hit to hit driver in a fairway more than 50% of the time. These players will usually have a rigid, straight forward arm in the backswing. This leads to less control of hitting a fairway. This is why you might see many players go for a 2-iron, 5-wood or 3-wood off the tee. Even with 5-woods, some of these players cannot consistently hit the fairway. Remember that the shorter the approach to the hole on the green, the easier the shot. I know what you might be thinking. Popular belief and traditional teaching will say something like a 50 yard pitch shot to a hole is harder than a full sand wedge, for example, from 100 yards. This is wrong. Hitting a shot from 50 yards will be easier to get it close to a hole for birdie or eagle on a par 5 then laying up and hitting a full sand wedge at 100 yards. Laying up on a hole from 100 yards instead of 50 yards is like adding another 50 yards to the golf course. If one was to lay up to 100 yards instead of 50 yards on a course, this would add approximately .23 to the course rating. This is calculated by dividing 50 by 220 ($50 \div 220$), which equals .227. If you round up this answer, it is .23. If a golfer lays up on all four of the par fives to 100 yards instead of 50 yards, they are essentially adding approximately one stroke to the course rating. This is calculated by multiplying .23 x 4 = .92, which is almost one stroke. This will add about a stroke to your score. This is one reason why the average score for amateurs has remained between 97 and 100 in the past 50 years.

The first hole on the course is a 400-yard par 4. If one hits the ball with driver for a drive of 160 yards, he has 240 yards left to the hole. He then proceeds to hit his 3-wood 145 yards. He now has 95 yards left to the hole. This would be an 8-iron. He lands it on the green and two putts for bogey five. If he elected to hit 3-wood off the tee, he would have had 255 yards left to the hole instead of 240 yards left. He would have hit another 3-wood from the fairway for a distance of 145 yards. Thus, his third shot would have been 110 yards from the green. This would have been a 7-iron. Using 3-wood off the tee would have added 15 yards to this hole. Of course, the third shot to the green would be 15 yards further away. Using 3-wood off the tee would have made the hole play like 415 yards instead of the 400 yards it was intended to play like. If this was done 14 times in a round, this would add approximately one stroke to your score.

This golfer is now faced with a 350-yard par 4. He uses a 3-wood off the tee and hits it 145 yards. Now he has 205 yards left to the hole. He hits another 3-wood and now has 60 yards left to the green. He hits this 60-yard pitch with his sand wedge and onto the green. He two putts for a bogey five. By not using driver off the tee, he made the hole play about 15 yards longer. This is because his driver goes approximately 15 yards further than this 3-wood. Now this 350-yard par 4 was playing at 365 yards. He now plays the same hole again, but this time uses a driver off the tee. He hits his driver 165 yards and now has 185 yards left to the green. He uses driver again from the fairway and hits it 155 yards. He now only has 30 yards left to the hole. He chips the ball to about 10 feet from the hole. He putts it in for a par.

Golfers that hit average drives of 180-200 yards

Mr. C's first hole on the course is a 360-yard par 4. If he hits the ball with driver and it rolls left of the fairway into the trees for a total of 200 yards, he still have 160 yards left to the hole. If he hits 3-wood instead on the tee and hits it in the middle of the fairway for a tee shot of 170 yards, he still has 190 yards to the green. When he takes an approach shot, he must use either a 3-wood, which will not get the ball there or a driver that is somewhat harder to hit off a fairway. If he uses driver on this approach shot and misses the green, bogey is likely. In any fashion, this is not an aggressive and productive way to play golf.

However, the ball hit with the driver that rolled in the trees will have a 160-yard approach instead. Say he has to pitch it out to 100 yards from the hole in order to out from under the trees. His third shot will probably not be close to the hole and bogey might be likely. What I am getting out here is that there is really no advantage to using a 3-wood off a par 4. If one hits driver to the middle of the fairway to 200 yards out, the approach shot is 160 yards instead of the 190 yards with the 3-wood. It is easier to get it on the green from 160 yards then from 190 yards. If one hits it in the trees from the tee with a 3-wood, the results would be more devastating. This is because the 3-wood would be even further away from the hole then the driver that was hit into the trees.

Golfers that hit average drives of 201-229 yards

If one hits a drive of 225 yards on a 510-yard par 5 and it goes in the fairway, there is 285 yards left to the hole. Now let us call this golfer, Mr. X. Mr. X now has a choice. Hit a 3-wood 200 yards, which will give 85 yards left to the hole or hit a 5-wood 180 yards, which will give about 105 yards to the hole. 105 yards just happens to be the perfect pitching wedge distance for Mr. X. Mr. X should rather hit a three-quarter pitching wedge at 85 yards because this distance is closer to the hole. Remember the closer to the hole, the more likely the birdie four is possible. Mr. X might get it on the green with the pitching wedge from 105 yards. However, the three-quarter pitching wedge from 85 yards is more likely to be closer to the hole. In fact, this shot will definitely guarantee par. It is very simple logic. When one putts, would you rather putt from 10 feet or 20 feet? Of course, 10 feet is more likely to go in than a putt from 20 feet. We should take care of our approach shots in the same way.

If Mr. X elected to hit 3-wood off the tee, he would be at a serious disadvantage. First off, the 200 yard drive of the 3-wood would leave 310 yards to the hole. Now hitting a 3-wood again on the second shot will leave 110 yards to the hole. 110 yards would be a little too long for his 105-yard length of his pitching wedge. Now he would have to hit a soft 9-iron. By hitting 3-wood off the tee, Mr. X added 25 yards to the length of this par 5 making it play at 535 yards instead of 510 yards. This is because hitting 3-wood took off 25 yards from his usual drive with the driver. Thus, the approach shot was made at 25 yards further out than when he used driver off the tee in the first example. The tee shot on a par 4 or par 5 is the foundation for what will occur. It is the most important shot for maximizing your chances at a birdie or eagle.

Golfers that hit average drives of 230-250 yards

If one hits a drive 240 yards with driver on a 450-yard par 4 and hits the fairway, there would be 210 yards left to the hole. Let us say this golfer is named Mrs. X. Mrs. X will now have a 3-wood approach to the hole. At least with using the driver off the tee, she is giving herself an opportunity to get the ball onto the green and to one putt for a birdie or two-putt for a par. If Mrs. X instead missed the green with her 3-wood approach shot 15 yards to the right, she must chip to the hole. The worse that might happen is a bogey five. However, if she chipped close enough, she most likely would get a par or even a birdie.

Now if Mrs. X elected to hit a 3-iron off the tee, she would have hit her tee shot 185 yards. This would have left her 265 yards to the hole. This would certainly take three shots to get it on the green. She would probably use 3-wood from 265 yards out and have 55 yards left on her pitch shot. She would use her sand wedge on this pitch shot to try to get it close to the hole for a chance at par. She pitches it to nine feet from the hole. See the kind of pressure this puts on Mrs. X just for getting par. By hitting 3-iron off the tee, Mrs. X puts herself at a defensive position from the start. However, using the strategy of hitting 3-iron off the tee on this long par 4 would usually lead to a bogey five or worse. In fact, using a 3-iron off the tee is adding an additional 55 yards to the length of this hole. Instead of this par 4 playing at 450 yards, it will now be playing at 505 yards. This long par 4 has now turned into a par 5 by using 3-iron off the tee.

Mrs. X now is about to tee off at a 485 yards par 5. She elects to hit a 3-wood off the tee. She hits it 215 yards. She now has 270 yards left to the hole. The ball is on a tight lie and she chooses to hit 3-wood again and hits it another 215 yards. She now has 55 yards left to the hole. She hits her sand wedge to about 3 feet from the hole. She putts it in for a birdie. This scenario might sound good since she got a birdie. However, there is even a better strategy. Mrs. X plays the same hole again. This time she tees off with a driver. She hits the driver 240 yards. This is 25 yards further than how far she can hit her 3-wood. She has 245 yards to the hole. She wants to hit her driver from the fairway; however, the grass is cut quite short. In this way, it would be impossible to hit the ball on the sweet spot of the driver. So instead, she hits her 3-wood and hits it 215 yards. She has now 30 yards left to the hole. In fact, the ball is only about 5 yards off the front of the green. She now attempts to chip the ball in the hole for an eagle. However, the chip was a little short and she has only 5 feet left to the hole. She putts the ball in for a birdie four. The point is that she only had a 30-yard chip to the hole for an eagle. In the previous example on this same hole, she had a 55-yard pitch for eagle. A chip at 30 yards is easier than a 55-yard pitch. The more opportunities one gives oneself for eagle, the easier it will be to get a birdie or par.

Golfers that hit average drives of 251-275 yards

Mr. College Golfer faces a 325-yard par 4. He is thinking about hitting his 5-wood off the tee instead of driver. He drives his 5-wood 215 yards off the tee. He has 110-yard approach to the green. Now he thinks he can take his wedge close enough to get a birdie. The result is that he gets the ball on the green but still has 15 feet to the hole. He two putts for par. Mr. College Golfer could have elected to hit driver instead. Since he averages drives of 270 yards off the tee, he would have had just a 55 yard pitch shot to the hole. It is much easier to get the ball closer to the hole at 55 yards then from 110 yards. Once again, think about how much easier it is to hole a 10-foot putt then a 20-foot putt. It really is common sense. From 55 yards, Mr. College Golfer would have increased his probability for a birdie three. Hitting an approach shot from a closer position than from a longer position is beneficial to maximize the lowest score possible on a hole.

Mr. College Golfer is about to play another hole, which is a 520-yard par 5. He hits a driver off the tee and hits it 240 yards on a fly and it rolls another 25 yards for a total drive of 265 yards. He now has 255 yards to the hole. He typically hits his 3-wood about 240 yards. He then lays up with his 9-iron and hits it 140 yards. He now has 115 yards left on his third shot. He uses a pitching wedge and hits the ball a little left of the green. He now has a 20-yard chip. He chips the ball to about five feet from the hole. He needs to make this putt for par. He misreads it and misses the putt. He now has a six-inch putt, which he routinely putts in for a bogey six. This did not have to happen. Here is a better scenario. Mr. College Golfer hits his driver off the tee and hits it for a total drive of 265 yards. He then uses his 3-wood for the second shot and hits it 240 yards. This gives him 15 yards left to the hole. His third shot is a chip of only 15 yards to the hole. He chips it to about 4 feet from the hole. He makes the putt and gets a birdie four. Since he used a 3-wood for the second shot, this puts Mr. College Golfer on the offensive. Laying up with the 9-iron in the previous example was setting himself for defensive golf. By hitting 3-wood on the second shot, he was chipping to the green for a possible eagle instead of chipping for birdie.

Golfers that hit average drives of 276-304 yards

A golfer is faced with a 567-yard par 5. The fairway is only 25 yards wide with no rough. He elects to hit a driver and hits it 290 yards on the left side of the fairway. He now has 277 yards for an approach. Although there is out of bounds 35 yards left of the hole, he hits 3-wood. However, there is no out of bounds or hazards right of the hole. He decides to hit 3-wood to the right side of the green, which is very smart play. Although the ball did not land on the green, it is only 30 feet in front of the hole. He is now chipping for eagle. It goes in. The worse that might have happened on this hole is getting a par five. A par five might have occurred if he did not chip close to the hole and then two-putted. However, the most likely situation is a birdie four. When one is chipping for an eagle, it is a little easier to relax then trying to get it close just to putt for a par. This is because going for an eagle or birdie always puts the golfer in an offensive position. Trying just to get it close to the hole to putt for par in this instance, puts the golfer in a defensive position.

If he decided to hit a 3-wood off the tee instead of driver because of the narrow fairway, he would have taken off about 30 yards off his tee shot. This in effect would be like adding 30 yards to the length of this hole. He hits 3-wood to 260 yards. Now he has 307 yards to the hole. He can hit the driver on the approach. However, it is much harder to get middle of the clubface contact with the ball since the fairway is cut short. This will ultimately lead to at least a 30-yard loss in distance with the driver. Now the approach shot with driver was hit 260 yards. He still has 47 yards left to the hole for the third shot. He chips it on the green to 15 feet from the hole and then two putts for a par. Using this strategy, he added about 30 unnecessary yards to this hole. This is calculated by adding 30 yards from the loss in distance using the 3-wood off the tee. This is equivalent to playing a very long 597-yard par 5. Hit driver on par fours and par fives to lower your score.

This same golfer is faced with a 302-yard par 4. There is out of bounds on the right. In addition, the fairway is about 25 yards wide. He chooses to hit a 7-iron instead and hits it 180 yards. He now has 122 yards left to the flag. He hits his pitching wedge and two putts for a par. This sounds good, right? Well, it could even be better. This golfer now goes back on the same tee and hits his driver. He hits it 280 yards on a fly, and it rolls to about 303 yards on the left portion of the green. He now has a 30-foot putt for eagle. He two putts and makes a birdie three. Even if he hit his drive to the greenside bunker, he would be still chipping for an eagle.

Hitting 7-iron off the tee put him at a disadvantage. This is because his second shot is 122 yards away from the green as opposed to hitting driver, which would be on the green or near the green. Hitting a putt or chip for eagle is much easier than going for eagle from 122 yards away. Hitting a 7-iron off the tee made the hole play 122 yards further. He actually made this short par 4 play at 424 yards by using 7-iron on the first shot.

Golfers that hit average drives of over 305 yards

Hitting the ball this far gives you a distinct advantage. You essentially should capitalize on every situation to get the most out of your distance. Let us call this golfer Mr. D. Mr. D. is faced with a 350-yard par 4. There is a large sand trap 30 yards in front of the green. The beginning of the sand trap to the hole is measured at 50 yards. Mr. D. must carry the ball 310 yards to hit it over the sand trap. However, he hits his 5-wood 250 yards instead off the tee. Now he has a 100 yard approach shot to the hole. This would be a nice, soft sand wedge. His approach shot is hit within 7 feet of the hole. He two-putts and makes par.

If Mr. D. elected to hit driver, it would have been a wiser choice. Mr. D. plays this par 4 again and hits his driver right into the sand trap in front of the green. The ball carried 295 yards and rolled into the sand trap for a total drive of 305 yards. Now Mr. D has an approach shot of 45 yards with his sand wedge from the sand trap. One might think this is not smart play because he is now in the sand. To the contrary, he is 55 yards closer to the hole then in the first example when Mr. D. hits his drive with the 5-wood.

He hits the ball to within 3 foot of the hole and birdies the hole. However, hitting the drive into the sand trap was really the worse thing that could have happened. If he used driver and carried the golf ball 295 yards a little left of the trap, the ball would have rolled another 25 yards for a total drive of 320 yards. This would have given Mr. D. only a 30-yard chip shot to the green. Now this would maximize his chances at a birdie or eagle. Although he landed in the sand trap, the worse thing that could have happened in this situation was two putting on the green for a par.

Mr. D is now faced with a 575-yard Par 5. He elects to hit driver and carries the ball 300 yards on the fly and it roles only 15 yards for a total drive of 315 yards because the fairway was a little wet. He now has 260 yards to the flag and instead of hitting a soft 3-wood, he elects to lay up with a 9-iron to about 100 yards from the green. He did this because he read somewhere that trying to hit a par 5 on the second shot is a high-risk shot. Therefore, from 100 yards, he hits a soft sand wedge and gets the ball within 10 feet of the cup. He putts and birdies the hole. Doing this strategy might seem the most logical way. However, it took eagle out of the question. What happens if he did not putt the ball in? He would be looking at a sure par. Mr. D. could have used his 3-wood for his second shot to the green and given himself a chance for either an eagle chip or eagle putt. Hitting a 3-wood is not a high-risk shot. This actually is the smarter shot. This is the smart, offensive play. Laying up to 100 yards for the third shot is like adding another 100 yards to this hole for Mr. D. This is because he could have easily got to the green with the 3-wood on his second shot. Instead, he chose to create an unneeded long third shot to the green. I call it long because if he missed the green with his 3-wood for his second shot, he would of had a chip 30 yards or less away from the hole for eagle. If he was really in control of the 3-wood, he could have got it on the green giving him the opportunity for an eagle putt. Mr. D. made the hole play at 675 yards by laying up to 100 yards from the hole. If he hit the 3-wood on the second shot, eagle was possible. Laying up to 100 yards made eagle out of the question unless Mr. D. holed the shot from 100 yards. However, this would not be likely.

Play with the course not against it

The golf course is really on your side when you follow the essentials described in the previous chapter. It is now time to unconsciously trust your swing. No matter how narrow the fairway or how small the green, the golf course will be less intimidating. Fairways are meant to guide you toward the best angle to the hole. Start looking at the course as your guide and not your enemy. The golf course will ultimately reward you for your job well done. Start to change your mindset. For example, start thinking that you can par every hole. In fact, take bogey out of the question. Set your expectations high. However, do this with little steps. For example, if your best score was 100, make 95 your goal. Once you reach 95 make 90 your goal and so on. Golf is a game of perseverance and discipline. It requires discipline by the way you practice. It requires perseverance to stick to your goals and not to get distracted by other things in life. Start planning your days more efficiently so you can fit in golf to your schedule. If you put the time in, achieving lower scores will be your reward. Golf is here to relax your mind and to give you a better quality of life. Basically, golf management is not an elaborate process that takes years of golf rounds to master. Use driver as much as possible on every par 4 or par 5. As one gets better in golf, the difficulty of each course will have less of an effect. For example, narrow fairways should appear less intimidating. Also, sand bunkers near the green will not be looked upon as threatening. In addition, hazards in front of the tee box will not give one doubts.

Footnotes

1. USGA is a registered trademark of the United States Golf Association, which was not involved in the production of, and does not endorse, this product.

Chapter 4

The Short Game as a Zero Handicap Golfer or Better

All chip shots around the green should be made with the sand wedge. Don't use three different wedges for different wedge shots. For example, don't use a 60 degree, 56 degree, and a 52 degree wedge for various chip shots around the green. Only use the typical 56 degree sand wedge. This will keep your game much simpler. Plus, your short game will improve much quicker than trying to learn three different chip shots since they are three different clubs with three different lofts and shaft lengths. Here is probably the most important aspect of your short game. Make sure to only chip with the toe of the club *(See figure 4.1)* from distances of 35 yards or

Figure 4.1. Chipping with the toe of the club will make it easier to hit from tight lies, rough and sand traps.

less from the hole. Chipping from the toe makes the ball come off softer. In this way, you will have more control. In addition, if you are in the rough, hitting from the toe will make the shot easier. Chipping from a tight lie in front of the green is always easy using the toe of the sand wedge. If you happen to be in a greenside sand bunker, also use the toe of the sand wedge. Hitting sand shots are easier when using the toe of the club. With sand bunker shots around the green, hit about one inch to two inches behind the ball. Only bring the club from one-quarter to half way back in the backswing. However, remember if the sand is wet and heavy you might have to hit about only one to one-half inch behind the ball. I also suggest not to hit from sand bunkers that have pebbles in them on a regular basis. These pebbles will scratch up your club and possibly are dangerous. I have seen some golfers get hit in the face with flying pebbles from their own sand shot. Some golf courses have cheap sand in their sand bunkers that are filled with pebbles (little rocks). Instead, try to hit out of sand that is white and fluffy. This is the good stuff. Professionals usually always hit from this white and fluffy stuff. It is much easier to hit a sand shot from this kind of sand. This is because the sand is more consistent. On the contrary, when the sand has pebbles in it, some parts of the sand might have more pebbles or less pebbles. This will make the shot easier or harder depending on what part of the sand your ball happens to be in. Don't have stiff wrists when chipping or putting the ball. Let your wrists move freely just like when your hitting a driver or an iron. If you use stiff wrists, you are diminishing the amount of "feel" in your short game. You will also find it harder to chip consistently. The short game is just a minimized version of the long game.

The Short Game Routine

Before putting, line up about 20 feet behind the ball to read the line of the putt. You are, or course, looking for breaks in the green whether the ball is going to go left, right, or straight to the hole. It is easier to read the green from 20 feet behind the ball than say from a shorter distance. When reading the green and you are 20 feet behind the ball, pick a spot on the green where you want to hit to. This spot is the point where the ball will start to curve into the direction of the hole. In other words, this is the perceived spot where you think the ball will start to break in order to get it in the hole. Once you pick this spot, visualize the ball rolling from this spot into the hole. You should visualize the ball without your eyes shut. Actually, look at that spot and see the ball going from that spot and rolling into the hole. Also, mentally hear the sound of this ball going into the hole. This spot is usually more than half way to the hole. However, it depends on how fast or how slow the green is. Now this spot is your first visual on the ball going into the hole. When you stand over the putt, you should make sure the ball is at the level of the inside forward foot, and then look at that spot again. See the ball roll from that spot and into the hole once again. Now when you are about to putt, you should think about hitting the ball slightly past that spot. This should help you get more putts in the hole. After a while this routine will be automatic.

When chipping, use the same visualization routine as with putting. This definitely makes us focus more on the target and easier to make more chips for birdies or pars. Always chip whenever possible around the green.

Chipping takes away most of the break of the green. So chip the ball as close as possible to the hole as long as it won't role past three feet from the hole. Chipping and putting require a lot of practice. The ability to read greens gets better over time and with experience. Resist the temptation of not reading your putts when practicing. Whether it is a two-foot putt or a 90-foot putt always read the expected path of the putt before putting.

Pitch shots are another important aspect of the short game. Pitch shots are made typically from over 35 yards to as long as 150 yards depending on how for you can hit your sand wedge and pitching wedge. If you can't hit a pitch shot more than 100 yards with your sand wedge, then hit the pitch shot with your pitching wedge. The pitch shot is a higher shot than the chip shot. The pitch shot normally goes higher because the club goes further back in the backswing. With chipping, the club might only go about a quarter way back in the backswing. Because of this, the ball doesn't go as high. Do not worry about the height. The height will take of itself. All you have to remember is that from 35 yards and under when around the green, use your sand wedge to chip it in the hole. Remember to use the toe of the sand wedge to chip the ball. For distances above 35 yards, use the center portion of the sand wedge clubface.

For sand bunker shots from the fairway that are 35 yards and above make sure you move a little closer to the ball in your stance. However, make sure you align the inside of your forward front foot with the ball. You are trying to hit the ball first before hitting the sand. Fairway sand shots require going down one club. So if you usually hit a pitching wedge from 110 yards and are faced with a 110-yard sand shot, take a 9-iron instead.

The Long Game Routine

The long game routine is pretty quick. When you are about to hit your drive, you should first place the ball on the tee. Then stand on the side of the ball where you take your stance. Before you take your stance figure out where you want to hit the ball. Is it on the right side of the fairway over a bunker? Maybe, you might want to hit it on the left side of the fairway over a tree for instance. Then align the inside of your front, forward foot with the ball. Now that you are in your stance, glance at the target you want the ball to go once again. When using driver off the tee, aim for something far away. Something like a tree that is, for example, 100 yards directly behind your target would be a good example. This will also maximize distance off the tee. Notice during the routine you don't have to go behind the ball to figure out where you want to hit it. Just go to the side. This is because you're not trying to read a green as in putting or chipping. You are just trying to figure out where you want to hit the ball. Practice swings before you hit the driver are only necessary on the first tee if you didn't warm up on the driving range before starting the round. However, I recommend against taking full practice swings before a shot. This is because if the practice swing doesn't feel right, you may feel less confident when you actually hit the shot. A half-practice swing is needed when you are about to hit a chip shot from the rough or a tight lie. In this way, you are checking to see the depth of the rough or hardness of the tight lie. In addition, when putting never take a practice putt stroke. The focus should be on the place where you want to putt to, not on how your putting technique feels. With driver and irons, the focus should be on where you want to hit the target. Taking practice swings distracts this focus and puts your thoughts on how your swing feels.

On a par 3, do the same routine as when you tee off with a driver. The only difference is that you should look for a target on the green. If the flag is close or at the middle of the green, you should use the flag as your target. However, if the flag is positioned on the side of the green, then hit it towards the middle of the green. This will increase the percentage of hitting the green in regulation. On a par 3, the goal is to get the ball on the green in one shot from the tee. If the ball gets close to the hole, that is great. You can get a birdie. Do not go straight for the flag when it is close to a hazard or located near either side of the end of the green. Aiming for the middle of the green increases the margin of error. Because if you hit it a little too far right, it most likely will still hit the green. If you hit it a little too far left, it might be close to the flag. In this case, you can putt it in for a birdie.

Where to Hit the Ball on Approach Shots

On approach shots, do the same routine. However, on approach shots on par fours from 36 to 100 yards you can be a little more aggressive. For example, a flag is on the left side of the green only four steps (12 feet) from the left edge. In this case, maybe hit the ball to the left center of the green instead of the center of the green. If the flag is only three steps (nine feet) from the front edge of the green, hit the ball approximately five feet past the flag for shots 75 yards to 100 yards. This will ensure that you hit the green in regulation. Once again, if you end up a little short, you can still be on the green. For shots of 36 to 74 yards, go right at the flag. At this distance, always go for birdie. When I say right at the flag, I mean attempt to hit the ball into the hole. This doesn't mean to try to hit the top of the flag with the ball. According to how fast or slow the green is, you might have to land the ball anywhere from two or more yards before the hole in order to possibly get the ball in the hole. This is because the ball will roll less or more once it lands on the green according to how much wind there is and how fast or slow the greens are. Here is a chart to follow for approach shots from 36 yards to 190 yards.

Position of flag	Approach shot yardage to the flag	Where you hit it
Center of green	36 to 190 yards	right at the flag
Right center or left center of green	75 to 190 yards	middle of green
Right center or left center of green	36 to 74 yards	right at the flag
Closer to left edge of the green then the to center of the green	75 to 190 yards	middle of green

Position of Flag	Approach Shot Yardage to the flag	Where you hit it
Closer to left edge of the green then to center of the green	36 to 74 yards	right at the flag
Closer to front edge of the green	36 to 74 yards	right at the flag
Closer to front edge of the green	75 to 190 yards	five feet past flag
Closer to back edge of the green	36 to 74 yards	right at the flag
Closer to back edge of the green	76 to 190 yards	hit slightly past middle of green

For approach shots that are over 190 yards go for the middle of the green. However, when there are crosswinds, you will have to adjust by hitting left or right of the green. In this way, the wind will push the ball into the center of the green.

Chapter 5

The Long Game as a Zero Handicap Golfer or Better

For many golfers, the long game might seem the most frustrating. For example, a golfer drives a ball perfectly down the middle of the fairway on one hole. Then on the next hole, this same golfer hits one out of bounds about 30 yards right of the fairway. This golfer can't understand why this happens. In fact, faulty technique is definitely the number one cause. However, many golfers don't attribute inconsistent golf to faulty technique. They attribute it to some kind of mystery. They believe that there are hot and cold streaks, and that there is no control over such streaks. I know that by using the essentials in this book with practice, hitting a driver can be a consistent process without succumbing to hot and cold streaks. There is no need for a hot streak because one can be consistent already. Thus, there is no need for a cold streak because with consistency there is a steadiness in the game. There is constancy and stability that makes golf more enjoyable to play. Playing with constancy, stability, steadiness and consistency is the best way to play the long game and of course every other aspect of golf.

When using your driver, always aim the ball to the center of the clubface. The center is where you will get most distance on your drives and on your fairway woods. Try to use your driver on every possible par 4 or par 5. This will help lower your score. Of course, if there is a lake that cuts off the fairway in the approximate distance of your driving distance, use another club. When using a driver, focus on the hitting the ball in the center of the club. Having a very slight pause at the top of the backswing is beneficial. This in some ways helps to give a consistent, smooth tempo in the downswing. I don't put this slight pause as one of the essentials because some players prefer a faster or slower tempo without a very slight pause. Tempo is always left up to the golfer. Every golfer has his or her own signature tempo.

Distance golf is probably one of the most enjoyable parts of the game. To hit a drive to a specific target that is only five yards wide feels very rewarding. To maximize distance off the tee is extremely beneficial. Frankly, the further one hits the ball, the easier it is to score lower. The shorter the golf course plays the easier it is to score well. It is easier to score lower from the forward tees than the back tees. This is because the forward tees make the course player shorter and the back tees make the course play longer. Using an iron off a par 4 or par 5 will make the course play longer. Of course, control of the golf ball is also another important element. However, it really is hard to hit a drive very far if you can't control the ball. When the ball is not in control, the ball slices or hooks rather harshly. With a controlled long drive, the ball either fades, draws or goes directly straight. One of the best feelings in golf is crushing a drive and really hitting that ball in the center of the clubface with ease. The longest drives are hit with less effort. Just swing as if you are hitting a short iron on an approach. The concentration is first on the target and then on getting that ball to hit the center of the clubface to propel that ball the maximum distance possible. Don't ever be afraid to use driver. Don't ever be afraid to use your 3-wood on the second shot on a par 5. Don't deny yourself the pleasure of truly crushing a drive. After using my techniques, some golfers might be able to hit a 3-wood to reach the green on their second shot. Other golfers might now be able to use an iron on their second shot to the green. Even some might now finally be able to get their third shot onto the green on a par 5. Whatever your skill level is right now, remember you can improve with practice, patience and self-discipline to stick to your golfing schedule. In fact, when I first played my first round of golf, my first golf score was 127. At that time, I was hitting severe slices and hooks. Although occasionally I could hit it straight, golf was quite frustrating. However, at that time I wasn't using the essentials of a zero handicap golfer or better. When using the driver, one should use a controlled aggression towards the ball. With practice, each drive can be hit solidly and as far as one can hit it.

Par threes that are over 200 yards require a certain amount of precision. Golfers might need to use anything from driver to a 7-iron. The aim on long par threes is to hit it on the center of the green. Resist going straight at a flag that is close to a sand bunker or water hazard.

Chapter 6

How to Practice Most Efficiently as a Zero Handicap Golfer or Better

Full Shots at the Golf Range

When practicing, don't hit any club more than once. However, you can go back to this club later in the practice session. Never use this club more than one time in a row. We are trying to simulate the conditions of actually playing on the golf course. Also, after each swing, keep changing the target to hit at and the club you are hitting with. You can hit at a specific target again a few swings later in your practice session. For example, first hit the ball to a flag 100 yards away to the right with your wedge. Then use your driver and hit directly at the 250 sign or flag that is straight in front of you. Always hit at a specific target. Keep the target small. Doing this strategy also practices your timing or tempo in the golf swing. If one hits driver on the golf range 20 times in a row, he or she is likely to suffer from increased muscle fatigue. This muscle fatigue can lead to inefficient techniques in the golf swing. However, constantly changing clubs at the golf range will give you a little break between swings, and this will decrease muscle fatigue. Remember if you practice like your playing a round of golf, you will lower your score at a faster rate.

Many times golfers hit a certain club too many times in a row in a practice session in order to attain perfection. I call this obsessive practice perfection. Yes, it is true, practice can make perfect but not in one session. Golf practice is a progression. So if you hit a 3-iron too far left of a target, don't obsess and keep hitting the 3-iron until you hit that perfect shot to the flag. Instead, just go on to the next club. Let go of that need for perfection. Perfection or near perfection can come with practice. Perfection will not come with obsessive practice. Inconsistent results in the golf swing from hitting the same golf club too many times in a row is referred to as *repetitive swing disorder*. This also occurs in baseball. When a hitter swings too many times without taking a break in his batting practice, this leads to muscle fatigue. This muscle fatigue can create a swing slightly different from the consistent swing, which can lead to a slump. It is better to go for near perfection when practicing. Go for a shot in the middle of the green. It's not always smart to go right for the flag. This is especially true when a near miss to the right will cause the ball to go into the bunker. If you really want to become a zero handicap golfer or better, practicing four times a week and playing one round of golf at least every other week is ideal. Here is what your practice schedule should be like.

Monday: Hit approximately 65 balls with full swing shots on the golf range using every club in the bag except the putter of course. Putt and chip 50 balls (chip 25 balls and putt 25 balls). However, make sure to chip five balls and then putt these five balls. Do this until you reach 50 balls total. One hundred fifteen balls are the total balls that are hit with full shots, chips and putts.
(Total Approximate Practice Time: 1 hour)

Tuesday: Day off from golf

Wednesday: Hit approximately 90 balls with full swing shots on the golf range using every club in the bag except the putter. Putt and chip 50 balls (chip 25 balls and putt 25 balls). However, make sure to chip five balls and then putt these five balls. Do this until your reach 50 balls total. One hundred forty balls are the total balls that are hit with full shots, chips and putts.

(Total Approximate Practice Time: 1 hour, 15 minutes)

Thursday: Putt and chip a total of 150 balls. Chip 75 balls and putt 75 balls.

(Total Approximate Practice Time: 1 hour)

Friday: Hit approximately 65 balls with full swing shots on the golf range using every club in the bag except putter. Putt and chip 100 balls (chip 50 balls and putt 50 balls). However, make sure to chip five balls and then putt these five balls. Do this until your reach 100 balls. One hundred sixty five balls are the total balls that are hit with full shots, chips and putts.

(Total Approximate Practice Time: 1 hour 25 minutes)

Saturday: Day off from golf

Sunday: Play a round of golf.

(Total Approximate Time: 4 hours)

Notice how you don't have to hit more than 100 balls with full swings at one practice session. There is no need for this with these techniques. Your schedule can be alternated with a round of golf on Monday instead of Sunday. Also, if you can't play a round of golf every week, play a round of golf at least 2-3 times a month. The main focus is to practice four times a week like it says in the schedule. Remember playing a round of golf also counts as practice. So count this as one of your four times that your practice in a week. Creating a schedule in your life and adhering to it will help achieve your goals. The aim in practice is balance, which is to give equal practice to every part of the game every week. It only takes 8 hours and 40 minutes per week for you to complete this golf schedule. However, some weeks that you do not play a round of golf, it will only take about 5 hours and 40 minutes a week to practice. This is because an hour of practice is substituted for the round of golf.

If it is too cold outside to play, go to a heated driving range. If it rains, try practicing indoors by only putting and possibly taking little chip shots. However, if in the house, make sure there is nobody around in the area of your practice. Always be safe when putting or chipping in the house. Make sure nothing is in breaking distance (i.e., furniture, windows). As a side note, it amazes me when I see people at professional golf tournaments stand so close to the flight of a player's ball. Professionals do make mistakes. They should never get close to the path of a professional or amateur's ball. If you can't chip in the house, make sure to take a 15 second brake after hitting five putts. This will help prevent unwanted bad habits when putting. If you practice like the schedule on the previous page, your score will get better and a zero handicap or better can be attainable with time. How much time you might ask? Well, it depends. I started to play golf when I was 23 years old. However, I only played for a couple of months and then stopped playing because of frustration and a lack of funds since I was a full-time student at the time. My first score was 127 at a Philadelphia municipal golf course. However, I did win a local long distance driving contest the first one I ever entered. I then started to play golf again at age 26. My second score was 117. I consider the age of 26 as my first year of playing golf because I only played golf for a couple of months when I was 23. However, my scores kept dropping in the first year. By the end of my first year of playing, my average score for the entire year was 97. My average score for my second year of playing was 89. This was the majority of the time playing from back tees with an average golf course rating of 73.5 and a slope of 138. I always encourage playing golf from the back tees if you're not already. It took me approximately three and half years to break 80. In fact, my average score for my third year on playing golf was 85.7. In my fourth year of playing, my average score was 83. In my fifth year of playing golf, I started to finish with my club high to the sky (this is essential #7 for the zero handicap golfer or better). My average score for my fifth year was 76.1. However, in the middle of my sixth year of playing golf, I was hitting approximately 60% of greens in regulation and about 61% of fairways. Therefore, instead of always setting up to the ball in the middle of my stance, I aligned the inside of my forward foot with the ball (this is essential #3 for the zero handicap golfer or better). I did this with driver and with every other club in my bag. This also includes the putter. This led to a dramatic increase in my greens in regulation percentage and fairways hit percentage. This led to an increase to about 82% of greens in regulation and 80% of fairways hit. I ended up with a 72.25 average in my sixth year of playing golf. However, in the second half of that year I was consistently shooting in the high sixties. This was because of essential #3. In addition, my driving distance went up 20 yards and my chipping and putting improved significantly. In my seventh year of playing golf, I had a 66.29 scoring average. My greens in regulation were 89% and 85% for fairways hit. I had four rounds that year where I actually hit 100% of the fairways. I also had two rounds that year where I hit 100% of greens in regulation. I wished I had figured out essential #3 earlier. This is because I would have improved at a much faster rate. Currently, I score in the low to mid-sixties. It goes to show you don't have to start at an early age to become very skillful at golf. If you can hit the ball at least 240 yards (carry and roll) on a drive, I recommend hitting from the back tees. You have a distinct advantage over me when I learned to play golf because now you have the knowledge of all the essentials of the zero handicap or better golf swing. This should accelerate your rate of improvement and can possibly make you a zero handicap golfer or better with time and practice.

Hitting full golf shots at the golf range can be rewarding. However, it is always more fun to hit drives on the golf course. They seem to go further on the golf course. Range balls actually do not go as far as the regular balls you use at the golf course. Range balls are usually meant for durability but not distance. Many range balls don't fly more than 260 yards even if you can fly one 330 yards with the golf ball purchased at a sporting good store. Range balls are usually very cheap to buy. They are significantly lower in price than the regular balls you buy at the sporting good store. Range balls are built for the golf range owner. Range balls are made to minimize loss. This is why they don't go nearly as far as regular golf balls. Also, don't get caught up with the distances at the golf range. Most golf ranges don't have accurate yardage markings. This is because grass ranges are constantly moving up or moving back the tee boxes. They are giving the grass a time to grow in a particular location where it is filled with divots. The main purpose is to hit each club to a specific target. Don't worry about the distances at the golf range. You should automatically hit the ball further on the golf course. Golf ranges are great for giving one access to hit at different targets. The main focus at the range is to concentrate on hitting the ball on the center of the clubface.

When hitting full shots, don't get discouraged by the unusually small greens found on many driving ranges. Greens on golf courses are in most cases bigger than the majority found on golf ranges. In addition, never practice chipping with range balls on the practice green. Use your regular balls when chipping and putting. An important purpose of chipping and putting is to develop feel with the balls you will use when playing on the golf course.

Chipping and Putting Practice

On the practice green, don't chip more than five balls in a row. Also, don't putt more than five balls in a row. You can chip and putt more balls in a row than in the full swing. This is because when chipping and putting, muscles are being used with much less force. Since there is less force, there will be less muscle fatigue. Therefore, the repetitive swing disorder is less likely to occur when chipping and putting. So in your practice session, chip five balls in a row to the same hole. Then putt these five balls. If you chip one of these balls in the hole, then only putt four balls. Keep track of this scrambling percentage. Scrambling percentage is the percentage one can get par or better from off the green in regulation. So since you are chipping from off the green, we are assuming that the green in regulation was missed if this was actual play. A par would be if you can chip and putt in two shots. A birdie would be if you chip into the hole in one shot. A bogey is if you chip and putt into the hole in three shots. Keep track of your statistics in this practice session. Each attempt at getting it into the hole is counted one time. For example, you chip to the hole and the ball lands three feet from the hole. You then putt this ball in the hole. This counts as a successful attempt. So now you are one for one. Now the next time you chip it to the hole it lands six feet from the hole. You try to putt in the hole from this distance but miss. This is an unsuccessful attempt. Now you would be one for two. In your third attempt, you chip the ball right into the hole. Therefore, you can't putt this ball since it is in the hole. This counts as a successful attempt. This counts as two for three. So do this for a total of 25 times. However, remember to never chip more than five times in a row and never putt more than five times in a row. After you chip and putt five times in a row, this is called an increment. After each increment, change the distance you chip from. For example, first chip five balls in a row from 20 feet from the hole. Then go to 15 feet, than to 25 feet. Then go to 30 feet. Finally, go to 15 feet again. Vary the distance in this way. This will be closest to course conditions. Once again, the main point is to vary the distance after each five chips in a row. If you can get it in the hole in two shots or less, this counts as a successful attempt in your scrambling percentage. If you get it in the hole in three shots or more, this counts as an unsuccessful attempt in your scrambling percentage. If you make 23 to 25 (92% to 100%) successful attempts, this is outstanding. If you make 20 to 22, (80% to 88%) this is excellent. 16 to 19 (64% to 76%) is very good. 12 to 15 (48% to 60%) is good. 8 to 11 (32% to 44%) is pretty good. 4 to 7 (16% to 28%) is fair. 1 to 3 (4% to 12%) is below fair. Keep in mind that approximately 65% is the highest scrambling percentage on the PGA tour. So don't be so hard on yourself. It takes time and practice. However, avoid believing that you won't reach anywhere near 65%. With practice and time, you might even achieve greater than a 65% scrambling percentage.

Since chipping to the hole will result in a decreased number of long putts, it is essential to also practice long putts between 15 to 60 feet in length. However, after practicing five separate long putts, make sure to switch to chipping. Chip another five chips. Although repetitive swing disorder is relatively low for putting and chipping, it still is better to keep practicing both parts of the game equally. This will promote consistency. With putts 30 feet or under, the goal is to make the putt and if you miss, have the ball roll no more than 17 inches past the cup. With putts 31 feet or longer, the goal is also to make the putt. However, if you miss, the ball should be within 3 feet of the cup. This will increase the probability of making the next putt.

Chapter 7

Playing Golf Shots Upwind, Downwind and Crosswind:
The Distance Your Golf Course is Actually Playing May Shock You

There is a big difference between how long a course is playing in the mornings and how it is playing in the afternoons, which are typically quite windy. Most people greatly underestimate the effect of the wind when playing. Not knowing how far a shot is actually playing because of the wind will guarantee higher scores. For example, on a par 3 over 200 yards into the wind, the majority of golfers will always make the mistake of hitting the ball way short of the hole. This is because the wind is underestimated. Here is a formula that can help in figuring out how far to play a golf shot in various wind conditions. Pick up about three to five blades of grass. From three and a half feet high (slightly above the height of the umbilicus or belly button), release them at your side. You then watch where the blades of grass land. Now from the point of release, step towards where the blades of grass landed. Then count each step. Each step should be approximately 3 feet in distance. Now times (multiply) the number of steps by 1.6. In a headwind (upwind), times this result by 3.9 when using driver if you can carry the ball between 150 to 223 yards. If you carry the ball between 224 to 299 yards, times the result by 5.1. If you can carry the ball between 300 to 320 yards, times the result by 6. If you can carry the ball over 320 yards, times the result by 6.5. In a headwind, using a 3-wood times the result by 3.9. In a headwind using irons times the result by 3.9. Here is an example:

A golfer is about to hit his driver into a pretty strong headwind. He releases the blades of grass and they land 5 yards behind him. Here is how you would figure it out:

5 x 1.6 = 8.0

8.0 x 5.1 = 40.8 yards

In other words, if he drove the ball normally 240 yards on the fly without wind, the ball will fly only 199.2 yards with this much wind in his face. It's amazing how much the wind has an effect on drives. This is why some days it may seem that the ball isn't going as far. The reason usually is that one is hitting into many headwinds and crosswinds on quite a number of holes.

Here is another example:

A golfer is about to hit a 3-iron into a very strong headwind. His normal carry distance with the 3-iron is 195 yards. He releases the blades of grass and they land 8 yards behind him. Here is how you would figure it out:

8 x 1.6 = 12.8

12.8 x 3.9 = 49.92 yards

This means that this golfer would lose 49.92 yards in carry distance into this headwind with the 3-iron. Therefore, his typical 195-yard 3-iron would only carry 145.08 yards into this wind. This is like adding 49.92 yards to a hole. So a typical par-3 hole measuring 195 yards will play 49.92 yards longer at approximately 245 yards hitting into this strong wind. Also, a par 3 hole measuring 147 yards hitting into this same strong wind will require a 3-iron for this golfer to hit and not hit typical 8-iron.

If you are hitting in a tailwind, which is downwind, times the result by 2.1 when using driver if you can carry the ball between 150 to 223 yards.

If you can carry the ball between 224 to 299 yards, you should times the result by 3. If you can carry the ball between 300 to 340 yards, you should times the result by 4.

A very small percentage of golfers can carry a golf ball over 260 yards on a fly with legal golf balls using drivers no more than 46 inches in length. When I say legal golf balls, I am usually referring to the balls you can buy at your local sporting good store or golf shop. In my experience, these are not juiced up balls. If hitting the ball downwind using irons, always multiply by 2.1. This is quite important. If hitting the ball downwind using 3-wood, multiply the result by 2.1. However, if you can carry the golf ball with your 3-wood over 250 yards, multiply the result by 2.9.

One is about to hit his 9-iron into a tailwind. His normal 9-iron length is 125 yards. He releases the blades of grass and they land approximately three yards in front of him. Here is how you would figure this out:

$3 \times 1.6 = 4.8$

$4.8 \times 2.1 = 10.08$ yards or approximately 10.1 yards

In other words, his 9-iron would travel approximately 10.1 yards further with this tailwind for a total carry distance of 135.1 yards. With time and practice, doing wind calculation should be easier. Knowing how the wind effects ball flight is important especially on approach shots during windy afternoons. Here is another example:

One is about to hit his driver into a tailwind, which is downwind. His normal driver carry distance is 285 yards. He releases the blades of grass and they land approximately 6 yards in front of him. Here is how he would figure this out.

6 x 1.6 = 9.6

9.6 x 3 = 28.8 yards

His driver would travel approximately 28.8 yards further with this tailwind for a total carry distance of 313.8 yards.

When playing into a crosswind, use the same formula as hitting into the wind (upwind). However, you divide the final answer by 2. In the previous example, the final answer was 28.8 yards. You would just divide 28.8 by 2 (27 ÷ 2 = 14.4 yards). Here is another example. A golfer must hit his driver into a crosswind on a 380-yard par 4. His normal carry distance is 225 yards. He releases the blades of grass and they fall 8 yards on the left side on him while facing the area of the intended flight of the ball. Here is how you would figure this out:

8 x 1.6 = 12.8

12.8 x 5.1 = 65.28 yards

65.28 yards ÷ 2 = 32.64 yards

His carry distance would be 32.64 yards less than his actual carry distance. His carry distance with the effect of the crosswind would be 192.36 yards.

After this golfer drives the ball 192.36 yards down the fairway, he still has 187.64 yards left to the hole. He thinks he still has the same crosswind speed from right to left. To make sure of this he does the same procedure. He releases the blades of grass and again they fall to his left. However, now they only fall 7 yards away. He elects to hit a 3-wood, which he can carry 200 yards on a fly in normal conditions without wind. Here is how he figured the distance.

7 x 1.6 = 11.2

11.2 x 3.9 = 43.68 yards or approximately 43.7 yards

43.7 yards ÷ 2 = 21.85 yards or approximately 21.9 yards

This means that his typical 200 yard carry of his 3-wood will only carry 178.1 yards on the fly. Since the hole is 187.64 yards away and the 3-wood might roll somewhat when it lands, 3-wood would be his optimal club to choose. Remember since there is a crosswind, the ball will not roll as much as in normal conditions without wind. He uses the 3-wood and lands on the front edge of the green, and it rolls right to the middle of the green towards the cup and stops two feet short of it. The actual yardage this hole played is 54.5 yards further or 434.5 yards. This is figured out from the result of the first example of 32.64 yards and the result of 21.9 yards from the second example on crosswind. 32.64 yards + 21.9 yards = 54.5 yards further. Then you just add 54.5 yards to the yardage of the hole (380 yards) and get an actual playing distance of 434.5 yards. Just think how much yardage this can add to the actual playing distance of a course if at least half of the holes on the course had this crosswind. Maybe if some had a crosswind and some had a headwind, the results could be even a greater actual playing distance. A headwind affects the golf ball much more than hitting downwind. In other words, a golf ball is more affected by hitting it into the wind. For example, hitting a golf ball into a 10 mph wind will affect the ball much more than hitting a ball into a 10 mph downwind. As for clubhead speed, here is a chart that measures the average carry distance in yards based on clubhead speed with driver at 80 degrees F at sea level. This is measured at optimal launch angles.

Clubhead speed with driver in miles per hour (mph)	Average carry distance in yards
60	140
65	150
70	160
75	170
80	180
85	190
90	200
95	210
100	220
105	230
110	240
115	250
120	260
125	270
130	280
135	290
140	300
145	310
150	320
155	330
160	340
165	350
170	360
175	370
180	380
185	390

The average carry for a drive among amateurs is approximately 190 yards on a fly. This is not the total driving distance. This 190-yard carry equates to an average clubhead speed of 85 mph. Using my techniques should increase your clubhead speed with driver. A typical golf drive has 25 yards of roll after it hits the fairway on a fly. This 190-yard carry should roll another 25 yards for a total of a 215-yard drive. Remember this occurs on a somewhat level fairway. However, the ball could roll less or more depending on how high you hit your drives. If you sky your drives, it might not roll more than 10 yards. If you hit line drive type drives, it might roll 35 yards instead of the average 25 yards. Some sources say that the average drive among amateur golfers is approximately 205 yards.[1] This is carry plus roll. Now to hit a drive of 300 yards (carry and roll), one must have at least 125 mph of clubhead speed. At 125 mph, the ball should carry to approximately 270 yards on a fly. Some fairways might roll out to 30 yards depending on how short the fairway grass is. So 270 yard carry plus 30 yards of roll would equal to a 300-yard drive. However, if this golfer was to hit on average fairways that roll the typical 25 yards, 125 mph might not be enough. The 25 yards of roll will only make the ball go to a total drive of 295 yards. In actuality, 127.5 mph is enough clubhead speed for a total drive of 300 yards. This amount of clubhead speed should carry the ball to 275 yards on a fly and roll another 25 yards for a total of a 300-yard drive. In order to be consistently hitting drives of over 300 yards, a golfer should have an average clubhead speed of 130 mph or over.

The ball roles less when you hit a ball from an elevated tee box. However, the ball will carry more from an elevated tee box. Every 10 yards the tee box is above the fairway, the ball will carry 10 yards more. If one is only five yards above the fairway, the ball will carry only five yards more. If one hits their drive 20 yards above the fairway, the ball will carry approximately 20 yards more. However, the ball will not roll as much when the ball is hit from elevated tee boxes. From experience, I have found the ball to only role about 15 yards instead of the 25 yards when hitting from an elevated tee from 10 yards (30 feet) above the fairway. On approach shots, every 2 yards the green is elevated, the hole will play approximately 2 yards further. If a hole is 20 yards (60 feet) above the fairway on the approach shot, it will play approximately 20 yards further. For example, a golfer has 140 yards to the hole. The hole is 12 yards (36 feet) above the fairway from where the golfer will take an approach shot. The shot will play 140 yards + 12 yards = 152 yards. This will cause the golfer to use a different club to get the ball to the hole on the elevated green.

People underestimate how far the course is actually playing. Here is an example of how a par 72 course that is measured at 6,729 yards with a Course Rating[®2] of 72.5 and a slope of 123 plays in afternoon windy conditions. The four par threes on the course play against the wind.

Normal playing length	Actual playing length in yards
180 yard par 3	225
152 yard par 3	190
220 yard par 3	275
175 yard par 3	215

Five par fours on the course play against the wind.

Normal playing length	Actual playing length in yards
360 yard par 4	450
410 yard par 4	490
440 yard par 4	505
290 yard par 4	360
425 yard par 4	502

Five par fours on the course play to a right crosswind.

Normal Playing length	Actual playing length in yards
320 yard par 4	345
400 yard par 4	450
410 yard par 4	460
432 yard par 4	502
380 yard par 4	430

Two par fives on the course play downwind.

Normal playing length	Actual playing length in yards
525 yard par 5	514
565 yard par 5	545

Two par fives on the course play against the wind.

Normal playing length	Actual playing length in yards
495	605
550	685

The actual playing length because of the wind is 7,748 yards. This is 1,020 yards longer than what the yardage says on the scorecard. According to a formula by the USGA, every 220 yards adds one stroke to the course rating (see Chapter 3). 1,019 yards ÷ 220 = 4.6 strokes. This 72.5 original course rating now plays to a 77.1 course rating. Notice how three of the four par threes play 215 yards or longer. In fact, now one par 3 has turned into a par 4 playing at 275 yards. Now that one par 3 is now a par 4, the course is now playing at a par 73.

The yardage on the scorecard has no par 4 playing more than 440 yards. After factoring in the wind, 7 out of the 10 par fours are playing 450 yards or greater. In fact, 4 of the 10 par fours are now par fives. A par 4 is defined as a hole that is measured at 251 yards to 470 yards. Three of the four par fours are playing more than 500 yards, and one plays at 490 yards. Now that four par fours are playing as par fives, the course is actually playing at a par 77.

The yardage on the scorecard has no par 5 playing more than 565 yards. However, after factoring in the wind, two of the four par fives are now playing over 600 yards. The two par fives that are playing downwind are not as affected by the wind as much as a crosswind or headwind. Both of these two par fives still play well over 500 yards for a legitimate distance. The other two par fives are actually playing like long par fives. These two par fives are playing at 600 and 685 yards. To sum up, this course with the effect of wind has three par threes, seven par fours and eight par fives. When it is windy in professional golf tournaments, the tees are moved up so the course plays as it is supposed to. You can do the same when it is very windy. You can move up to a forward tee box on very long par fours when the wind is making it play like a par five. This may help to keep it playing like a par four or just leave the par four as it is. Remember to write the actual yardage on the scorecard the hole is playing like in windy conditions.

When courses are rated, they are usually rated in very good conditions. This is usually in the spring or summer, in the morning and with minimal or no wind. The greens role beautifully, the fairways are moist enough to hit from but not too wet where roll is severely limited. The entire course is maintained properly. These are optimal conditions. USGA course ratings are based on the course at optimal conditions. Most courses in the United States play much harder in the afternoon then in the mornings because of the windier conditions. Some golfers feel they are not improving if they score the same score in the morning one week in optimal conditions and the same score in the typical afternoon conditions the next week. In fact, as shown in the previous sentence, the scores did improve. For instance, if one golfer's course played to a course rating of 71.0 in the morning and a factored in 74.5 course rating in the afternoon due to windy conditions, he did improve a lot although he has the same score. If this golfer scored an 85 in the morning with the 71.0 course rating and an 85 with a 74.5 course rating in the afternoon, he improved by approximately 3.5 strokes. This would be like scoring an 81.5 in the morning in optimal conditions. Here is a summary chart for male golfers that corresponds to what yardage equals in regards to par at a particular hole.

Par 6	690 yards and greater
Par 5	470 yards to 689 yards
Par 4	250 yards to 469 yards
Par 3	249 yards and less

Here is a summary chart for the female golfer that corresponds to what yardage equals in regards to par at a particular hole.

Par 6	575 yards and greater
Par 5	400 to 574 yards
Par 4	210 to 399 yards
Par 3	209 yards and less

Remember that the lady tees will have lower start off yardages for par threes, fours, fives and sixes. One case of argument is what you might see on television. A 500-yard hole listed as a par 4. In fact, even at your home golf course, you might see 620-yard par fives. Local golf courses do eventually copy the par length of what golf courses are shown on television in professional events. Stick to this chart when evaluating your course in windy conditions. In the previous example of the golf course yardages in windy conditions, keep statistics of your scores with the different course ratings. In other words, if you score 79 when you play your golf course in windy conditions, this will change the course rating of the course. Use the new course rating with the 79 score to keep tract of your statistics. If the original course rating is 71.5 and a Slope Rating[®3] of 126 and in windy conditions you figure out the course to be playing at 76.0, your 79 score should be listed in this way. List the 79 score under 76.0 course rating and keep the same slope rating® of 126. I say keep the slope rating® because it is extremely complicated to try to figure out the new slope rating based on windier conditions. According to the USGA, you must always post scores using the exact course rating that is on the scorecard. However, this may seem unfair because the course many times is playing harder. However, if one is going to follow USGA rules, one must abide by them when posting scores for handicap purposes only. This is another reason why some people in amateur tournaments have an advantage. For example, a golfer who only plays golf in the afternoon when his course plays harder has a handicap of 10. Another golfer who only plays golf in the mornings in calm, optimal conditions has a handicap of 10 also. In actuality, the first golfer really has a lower handicap because he is playing in harder conditions where the course rating is significantly increased. The second golfer plays when the golf course is pretty much near the course rating. He is the actual 10 handicapper. The first golfer is probably around a 6.5 handicapper. Both golfers will get the same 10 strokes subtracted to their gross score in a handicapped sanctioned event. However, I still do recommend getting a handicap. It is still a wonderful tool for assessing one's improvement on different golf courses.

Footnotes

1. Average Driving Distance of Double-Handicappers, USGA July 2, 2004.

2. Course Rating is a trademark or registered trademark of the United States Golf Association, which was not involved in the production of, and does not endorse, this product.

3. Slope Rating is a registered trademark of the United States Golf Association, which was not involved in the production of, and does not endorse, this product.

Chapter 8
The Common Myths in Golf

There have been myths in golf that have been taught for many years. These myths are in existence because of the overwhelming conformity that is witnessed today. Golfers have followed these myths blindly on the premise that they will improve if they follow them. Another methodology is to always keep doing what has been done. If it has given some golfers moderate results, why not use them. In order for one to reach their specific potential, one must go above what always been believed or thought. After all, it has been said that the majority is often wrong. If one wants to achieve excellence in golf, one must be open to new ways of thought. We are not striving for moderate and mediocre results. We are striving to fulfill our total potential by improving at a faster rate. Here are some common myths of golf that will be explained and exposed.

Myth #1: Add width to your backswing.

This one seems to make sense from a logical standpoint. For example, a 48-inch driver will hit the ball longer than a 45-inch driver will. This is because the 48-inch driver has a longer shaft. This is applied also to some techniques in regard to keeping the forward arm in the backswing straight without bending the elbow. This also includes keeping it straight at the top of the backswing. Keeping the arm straight will supposedly maximize the length of the arm. The theory is to keep your arm straight or extended to increase the width of the swing. This is thought to increase clubhead speed. However, humans are not golf clubs. In fact, muscles are not stronger in extension positions at the top of the backswing. Muscles are stronger in flexion positions. This is why one should always bend their front arm at the top of the backswing **(Essential #4)**. If a golfer keeps the forward arm straight at the top of the backswing, this will decrease power. The arms should be extended right when the clubface is hitting the ball. However, the bulk of the clubhead speed is generated by bending the elbow in the backswing. Humans are not robots or things like golf clubs. Hitting a golf ball like a robot does not make sense. Human muscles don't work like something mechanical, which is man-made. For example, baseball pitchers always bend their arm at the elbow to throw a pitch. Yes, they eventually extend their arm at the end of the pitch but the bulk of the power is generated by bending the elbow. If they kept their arm straight during the entire motion, the speeds of their pitches would be greatly reduced and with much less control. A baseball hitter also bends their arm at the elbow in their backswing. Tennis players also bend their arms at the elbow when they take their tennis racket back. Hence, keeping the forward arm straight in the backswing in golf will cause too much stress on the muscles of the shoulders. This eventually can lead to joint pain in the shoulder. More power can be build up by bending the forward arm at the top of the backswing.

Myth #2: Avoid using driver if you don't have to when playing a round of golf.

If one doesn't use driver, the golf course will play longer. By doing this, you are turning long par fours into par fives. Regarding par fives, they will even play longer. In fact, the correct advice is the following: use driver as much as possible on the golf course. The only way to get more consistent with the driver is to use this club. If you avoid using it, you will have less consistent rounds with the driver in the future. Thus, this will hinder improvement.

Myth #3: Substitute the driver with the 3-wood. Using the 3-wood will give you more control on drives.

Substituting the driver with the 3-wood will take 25-30 yards off your drives. If one does this 14 times a round, one will increase the course rating by 1.9. This is calculated in this way. 14 drives x 30 yards = 420 yards. Then $420 \div 220 = 1.9$. A course with a course rating of 73.0 in optimal conditions will now play at 74.9. How much more control a 3-wood gives on drives is also minimal. It is a matter of practice. You can have as much control with your 3-wood as your driver. Once again, every club in your bag should be perceived as having the same skill level to hit.

Myth #4: Chip the ball in a way to make it land as fast as possible to maximize roll to the hole.

This is wrong because now one would have to contend with more breaks (curves) in the green. This is like giving oneself a long putt instead of a shorter one. Instead, chip the ball as close as possible to the hole. Do this as long as the ball will not role past more than three feet from the hole. There are two reasons for chipping. The first one is to chip the ball into the hole. The second reason is to reduce the length as much as possible of the next possible putt.

Myth #5: You should chip and putt with stiff wrists.

Actually doing this will reduce "feel." This is like trying to swing like a robot. We are not designed like robots. Let your wrists move freely and this will lead to greater improvement and lead to greater "touch" around the greens. The short game is just a minimized version of the long game. The only difference is the much shorter backswing and follow-through involved in putting and chipping.

Myth #6: In order to shoot a really low score, one must go straight at every flag on approach shots.

This is simply false. In fact, going for every flag will lead to higher scores. The main goal on approach shots is simply to get the ball onto the green. Greens hit in regulation is probably the most significant statistic that correlates well with low scores. Frankly, if you get the ball on the putting surface (the green) by hitting the green in regulation, you are always giving yourself an opportunity for birdie, par or even an occasional eagle. I'm not saying you cannot chip in for birdie, par or eagle. However, most golfers will make more birdies and eagles when putting then chipping them in from off the green. This is because when hitting a green in regulation, you might hit the ball three feet from the hole. This would be an easy birdie on a par 4. However, if you missed the green in regulation, you probably will be at least 10 feet or more from the hole. It is easier for most golfers to hole a three-foot putt than a 10-foot or more chip. The whole strategy to hitting more greens in regulation is to play consistent. Avoid going straight for sucker pins that are close to sand bunkers or water hazards.

Myth #7: Taking the club past parallel in the backswing can give you more power.

This is false. Taking the club past parallel in the backswing is an unnecessary movement. In fact, doing this will only create a longer path back to the ball, which can lead to inconsistent results. The essentials in chapter 2 will prevent this from happening. Remember power is first generated by the weight shift. According to the essentials of the zero handicap golfer or better, don't even go to parallel in the backswing. The shorter length of the backswing in a zero handicap golfer or better contributes to a shorter path to the ball when hitting it. Thus, you will have greater control, consistency and even more power.

Myth #8:   Lifting weights will hurt your golf swing and lead to inconsistency.

Lifting weights will not hurt your golf swing. This myth was probably proposed by one who had started to lift weights for a couple of days and noticed how tight his muscles were when he went out to play golf. This person stopped weightlifting because he thought it would make him too tight and mess up his swing. In actuality, the first week of starting a weightlifting program can contribute to sore and stiff muscles. However, this soreness and stiffness should go away after the muscles get used to the consistent routine of lifting weights three times a week. Actually, lifting weights will make one stronger and contribute to greater clubhead speed along with stretching after lifting. This equates to more distance off the tee. As an example, when I started lifting weights three times a week, muscle stiffness and soreness went away after about 10 days. With some people, it can be fewer days and other people a few more days before the muscle stiffness and soreness subside.

Chapter 9

The Mental Aspect: What to Do Before Hitting the Golf Ball

Frustration is sometimes part of any endeavor worth pursuing. Whether one has an injury that prevents him or her from playing golf that day, it has to be dealt with patience and time. However, using these techniques in this book should keep frustration at a minimum. This is because through practice and time, you should improve on a consistent basis from month to month and from year to year. There are some things to avoid in the thinking process out on the golf course. If one hits a bad shot, he should avoid beating himself up mentally. If one said things to himself like "I'm not good enough" when things didn't go his way, this will make his path to improvement slower.

Some golfers suffer from lack of confidence when playing in front of other people. These golfers get really self-conscious over every shot. The truth is the other players in their group really don't care how he or she plays. Yes, the others might seem like they care when they give their obligatory "nice drive compliment" when a drive goes down the middle of the fairway. However, they really don't. Most are caring about how they are playing and not care less about how the others are performing. The only way another golfer might care is when they are making comparisons between themselves and the other players. This caring is self-centered again. They want to see how good they are compared to the other players in the group. There is one exception to this. People who really care are the ones who really love you unconditionally. They are not coming from self-centeredness. They really want you to do well.

In our society, everything seems to be a competition nowadays. Examples vary from who can hit the ball the furthest to who has the prettiest house. People would be much happier if they stayed away from always making everything a competition. If everyone helped each other, instead of always competing against each other, people would be happier and the distribution of wealth would be more balanced. Anyway, don't feel added pressure when playing with other golfers. They really don't care about how you play. So playing with other golfers should be looked upon as playing a round by yourself except the round might take somewhat more time to play. If you perceive playing golf with others as really just playing by yourself, as a single, you won't feel any added anxiety. In fact, you will score just as well when playing, either as a single or with other playing partners.

A beneficial aspect about playing good golf is letting go of your ego. I describe the ego as related to golf as the part of the mind that wants to show off one's skills in front of others. In this way, the ego makes the false assumption that playing really good impresses others and thus, shows one's superiority to others. The competitive nature of the ego is quite anxiety producing. The ego is demanding one part of the golfer's brain to play perfectly, out drive the playing partners, hit every green in regulation and of course make every putt. In this way, the golfer's ego feels that this is a way to prove his superiority to others. The whole purpose of needing to be superior is to prove to oneself that he or she is a worthy person. Many golfers equate their golf performance as a measuring scale to measure how much they like themselves. So if one does well one day, he likes himself. If he plays poorly, he doesn't like himself. This is why some golfers may quit playing golf. The feelings are sometimes so painful of not liking oneself during a flurry of bad rounds that quitting golf seems to be a safe alternative or maybe just declaring golf a stupid sport. This way the golfer shifts the blame to something else. The golf ego puts tremendous pressure on oneself to achieve. When someone cannot perform at his or her highest level in a crucial part of the round, the golfer is described as choking. I think the term "choking" is much too critical. Choking occurs when the golfer puts too much pressure on oneself to achieve. This pressure is directly caused by the ego. Since the ego wants the person to be perfect and superior in all circumstances, this is unrealistic. When a golfer does a little mistake like missing a short putt, the ego might put self-thoughts in the golfer's head like, "if you can't make that small putt, how do you expect to make the longer putts." So when the golfer needs to make another putt, he fails because of this negative self-talk. The golf ego is sometimes responsible for the feeling of embarrassment or shame that takes over when not playing well. This is because the ego is mainly interested in the false perception that his playing partners or the audience needs to be impressed by his golf game. Again, people really don't care. The ego wants to impress because it thinks that achievement in golf will impress others. In this way, this golfer will value himself based on how well he is achieving.

Here are some examples of how the ego actually hurts the golfer's game. A 10-handicap golfer is faced with a narrow fairway that is 25 yards wide on the first tee. He wants to impress his playing partners and so wants to hit the longest drive. His ego has taken over at this point. The ego is a perfectionist and will not have any patience for anything less. In fact, the ego is about all-or-nothing. He hits a drive of 275 yards to the left side of the fairway. However, one of his playing partners out drives him by 10 yards. At this point, this 10-handicap golfer now feels inferior to the other golfer. Not only did he drive about 30 yards less than his average drives, he now was out driven. This is not being perfect or superior according to his ego. However, the 10-handicap golfer being controlled by his ego did not concentrate on hitting the ball in the center of his clubface. Instead, he hit the ball closer to the toe of his clubface. Being so obsessed with perfection, he forgot to concentrate on what he was doing. In this way, his ego paralyzed his concentration. His ego was more focused on the future result of hitting his average drive of at least 305 yards than being in the present and concentrating on hitting the ball on the center of the clubface.

A zero handicap golfer is faced with a four-foot putt for the win at a local golf tournament. His golf ego tells him you must make this or you are no good. His ego thinks that other people watching will think he is no good if he misses the putt. This is because once again his ego falsely thinks that he needs to impress others. This zero handicap golfer misses the putt. He goes on in a sudden-death play-off and loses the tournament because of his opponent, the ego. This zero handicap golfer would have greatly increased the probability of making this putt by letting go of his ego. His self-talk should have been like this, "if you hole this putt, that is great. However, if you don't that's ok, too." The important thing is that you did your absolute best to make this putt." Having the ego maintain control of a golfer is not the absolute best he or she can do.

A +5 handicap golfer watches one of his playing partners hit a 3-wood 275 yards on this second shot to the green. The ball lands five feet from the cup. This definitely looks like an easy eagle. Now this +5 handicap golfer has 290 yards to the green on this second shot. However, there is now a stronger wind that he must hit into. Also, there is a large water hazard straight in front of the green. His ego wanting to show his superiority, insists on using 3-wood also. This will guarantee superiority (in his ego) if he can get it on the green and get it less than five feet from the cup. He swings and the ball lands 40 yards short of the green and into the water hazard. He is now only looking at a par at best or most likely a certain bogey. The wind got stronger in his face and, thus, he should have played a safer shot. This is because the wind made his 290-yard distance to the green play about 330 yards. His golf ego made him think illogically. Here is a chart with words that are based on ego. The healthy words should replace the negative ego words.

Ego Words	**Healthy Words**
Perfectionist- I must hit every drive perfectly and hole every possible putt.	If you don't do your best, that's ok. If you do your best, that's ok, too.
I want to impress others.	There is no need to impress others since others really don't care how you perform.

Ego Words	**Healthy Words**
All-or-nothing golf shots. If I hit a drive over 250 yards, I'm great. If I don't, I'll feel inferior.	Golf is about leaving your ego behind so you actually can play your best.
If I don't win, everyone will think I'm a failure.	Well, if someone did feel this way about you, they are not really your friends anyway.
If I'm unable to perform well, my self-worth will suffer.	Separate your self-worth from your golf ego. Doing this will help you play better golf. Your performance in golf has nothing to do with your self-worth as a person in this world.

Every Day Can be a Good Day in Golf

It is true every day can be a good day. In other words, using these techniques in this book can possibly make every day a good day in golf. There is no need for slumps. Slumps do not have to be a part of life in golf. Many golfers have the mindset that there are going to be good days in golf and bad days. As if nobody can escape it. In reality, nobody must have bad performance days in golf. Slumps do not have to come. Change your mindset of what conventional golf has told us. One can be constantly consistent at golf. In fact, the essentials in Chapter 2 of this book are geared towards consistency. The essentials are designed to be a golfer's prevention against slumps. When you are out at the golf course, perceive every hole as a possible definite par and possible birdie. This is true whether you are playing a 460-yard par 4, a 120-yard par 3 or a 560-yard par 5. When you get to the point of being able to par every hole on the course with ease, now make birdie what you see as par in your mind for yourself. Higher expectations and goals will also make one improve at a faster pace. If one does this strategy, this will increase the probability of making birdie or even eagle. Also, the pars will now be looked upon as a bogey. When a golfer gets to the point where they can really perceive getting a par as a type of bogey, this golfer is what I call a master golfer. This is because birdie or eagle is what this golfer is striving for at every hole. In fact, this golfer might feel like he lost an opportunity to lower his score if he scores a par on a par 5 or a par on a short par 4.

Being a master golfer takes steps. First, make the short par fives and short par fours the main goal for getting birdies on. Second, make the long par fives and long par fours the next goal for getting birdies on. Third, make the short par threes another goal for getting birdies on. Finally, make the long par threes the ultimate goal for getting birdies on. If one can get consistent birdies on par threes that are over 200 yards, one truly has conquered golf. I think having low expectations is not the best measure for increasing the rate of improvement in golf. Many golfers may have no goals to prevent them from getting disappointment if they do score poorly.

However, having higher goals will gear one in the right direction, which is towards lowering his or her score. Write your goals on paper or type them onto your personal computer. If you are an 18-handicap golfer and want to be a 15-handicap golfer by next month, your goal can appear like this. For example, say your name is Mr. X Golfer and the next month is December. Write this. Mr. X Golfer will be at least a 15-handicap golfer by the end of December 20__ (fill in the year also). Do you see how this is written? The words "at least" are important because it leaves also the possibility of Mr. X Golfer having a handicap lower than 15. It is important to be as specific as possible. Always put the month and year in your goal. The time must also be entered in a goal. Another goal could be to write down that you want to increase your driving distance by 10 yards and Mr. X Golfer's driving distance currently is 255 yards. This type of goal would be written like this. Mr. X Golfer's (put your real name) average driving distance is at least 265 yards by the end of January 20__ (fill in the year). Writing down or typing down goals into your computer can greatly increase your efficiency in reaching your goals. If you don't reach the goal in the time you have written down for, avoid getting discouraged. Sometimes goals take a little more time. However, some goals you write down make actually take less time to achieve then you have thought. In this way, they even out. Some goals are achieved in less time and some goals may take more time to achieve. Keep the old goals you achieve, and write down next to them that you have achieved them. Another goal could also be stated like this. Mr. X Golfer (put your real name) will hit at least 50% of greens in regulation by May of 20___ (fill in year). In this way, you are guiding yourself to what you want to accomplish. The written and the spoken word have a lot of power. Be careful what you say and write about yourself. Avoid negative comments like "I'm stupid" or "I'm not talented enough" when speaking. These kinds of comments even in humor should be avoided. If you want to go against yourself and improve at a slower rate, putting yourself down is the surest way to go. If you want to getter better at a faster rate at golf, you should have positive thoughts about yourself. Start saying, "I can achieve what I want in golf." Also, avoid comparing yourself with others. For example, if you're a 15-handicap right now and look upon a zero handicap golfer as something unattainable, you will find it very hard to get this level. Forget what other people might tell you and how impressed they are with other highly skilled golfers. In fact, you don't even have to tell people what your goals are. Sometimes keeping them private eliminates unneeded judgment from others. You might be surprised that even family members might even think your goals are crazy or unattainable and might even get jealous of your accomplishments. Dare to imagine. There are no limits. The limits are in our brains. Listen to yourself. Many times the majority is wrong on many issues.

Chapter 10
Prevention from Injury

Many injuries can occur in golf. However, prevention is key to avoiding injury. When you finish high in the follow-through, make sure you don't have a reverse "C" in the lower back area. *(See Figure 10.1)*

Figure 10.1. This is incorrect. There is a reverse "C" in the backswing in the lower back.

Figure 10.2. This is correct.

This demonstrates excellent posture in the follow-through. Notice there is no arching of the lower back area (no reverse "C").

In other words, don't arch your lower back in the follow-through. *(See Figure 10.2)*. This may eventually cause low back pain and injury to the discs in the lower back over time. This is because rotating and hyper-extending your low back may cause injury to the facet joints in the lower back area also. Having a reverse "C" in the lower back area at the end of the follow-through is an unnecessary move. Doing this does not lead to more power. In fact, it throws one off balance and leads to inconsistency in hitting fairways and greens in regulation. Proper stretching before practicing golf is always required to insure one doesn't strain their muscles or sprain their ligaments.

When on the golf course or golf range and your ball is sitting on a piece of very hard ground, I advise just using a tee. Hit the ball off the tee. This will help protect your wrists from ligament damage. These hard surfaces usually occur on golf courses in the summer when some courses are not watered enough to keep up with the powerful sun. These hard surfaces often have dried out dead grass on them or hardly any grass on them at all. In other cases, there might be a small hint of grass and dirt together. Hitting the ball on a hard surface (feels like a hard floor) puts tremendous stress on the wrists, especially the forward wrist. Hitting the ball from the tee is better than hurting your wrists and not being able to play because of injury. If the course is not fit to play and one must use tees on approach shots, one should avoid counting this round as one of his scores. Sometimes it might be better to pay a little more for a better maintained golf course than to hurt one's wrist or shoulder joints. Professional golf tournaments don't use courses where the fairways are as hard as rocks. These fairways are perfect and are easy on the wrists. Avoid playing on a course that will make your score inflate because it is poorly maintained. Golf can be expensive depending on where you live. However, playing golf in the afternoons at the twilight rate can reduce costs. Many golf courses reduce the greens fees by one-half the price for an afternoon tee time. Many times a well-maintained course is much cheaper to play in the afternoon. In addition, the golf course is usually less crowded in the afternoon. I always like playing when there are fewer golfers on the course. A five hour round in the morning can sometimes be only two hours and forty-five minutes in the afternoon if you play by yourself and the course is not crowded. I think a lot of golfers stay away from playing in the afternoons because it is windier making the course play much longer. Now that you know how to figure out various wind conditions (see Chapter 7), playing in the afternoon will be more fun.

Now I'm going to discuss the importance of sunblock. Sunblock should be used every time one plays golf. It should be applied to the following areas before going outside: back of neck, front of neck, sides of neck, ear lobes, on the face, arms and legs if one wears shorts. It is also advisable to play in pants then in shorts. This way you won't need to apply as much sunblock. Also, when out in the sun wear an undershirt under your regular golf shirt. This will give added protection. Some shirts are way too thin to give enough protection against the sun. Darker shirts give more protection against the sun than lighter shirts. It is also advisable to wear a v-neck tee shirt under the golf shirt. This will give you added protection against the harmful rays of the sun. In addition, a wide brim hat is also a good idea. This helps to reduce fatigue because it protects the head from the intense sunrays. The hat is also another added protection against the sun along with the sunblock. Never substitute a hat for sunblock. To protect the hands, I advise wearing two golf gloves. Wear one on the right hand and one on the left hand. Use sun block with a SPF of at least 40 in the summer and an SPF of at least 30 in the winter. Make sure you use a sunblock that protects against both UVA and UVB rays. This way you can be protected against both premature aging and sunburns. Not protecting your skin with sunblock in the sun increases one's chances of getting skin cancer. Basal cell carcinoma is the most common type of skin cancer. Lesions can appear in an array of colors. Most cancerous lesions are irregular in shape; they are not symmetrical. In other words, most cancerous lesions are usually not circular in shape. Basal cell carcinoma is a type of cancer that rarely spreads. Malignant melanoma is the most deadly form of skin cancer. This is because this type rapidly spreads from a cancer of the skin to other parts of the body. According to many sources, most cancerous lesions are usually raised and irregular in shape. Most non-cancerous lesions are usually flat in appearance. [1]

UVA rays from the sun are responsible for premature aging and some skin cancer. UVB is also responsible for sunburns, premature aging and most skin cancers. Wearing a sunblock with certain ingredients is important to protect against these rays. Also, remember UVA ray concentrations are in equal amounts through out the year. UVB is usually stronger in the summer months. UVA rays can also penetrate car windows. This is why it is important to wear sunscreen whenever you go out in the daylight. Zinc oxide is considered one of the best ingredients in a broad-spectrum sunblock. Many sources also say that octocrylene, benzophenone-3 (oxybenzone) and octyl methoxycinnamte are ingredients that are very good protection from the sun. I have used sunblock with these ingredients and found them to protect me from the harmful rays of the sun.

When at a driving range, try hitting only from grass. Avoid hitting on artificial turf. Artificial turf many times sits on concrete and can be quite hard on the body to hit on. For one, the wrists, elbows and shoulders are more at risk of injury when hitting on such a surface. However, I know some driving ranges only have artificial turf. In this case, always use a tee when hitting on artificial turf. If you're hitting driver, use the rubber tee found at the range. If you are hitting an iron, use a shorter tee. Hitting from a tee may help prevent injury when hitting off artificial turf at the range.

When walking the golf course instead of riding, avoid carrying your golf bag on your back with the double strap (same position as carrying a nap sack). Many golf bags weigh over 25 pounds, and this puts too much stress on the lower back. For one, walking with a golf bag on your back makes your lower back hyperextend. In this way, this can damage the joints and discs in the lumbar area (low back) of the spine. Also, carrying a bag of clubs will tire you out much quicker. This can lead to increased mental and physical fatigue, which sometimes is detrimental to scoring well. In addition, avoid carrying the golf bag on one shoulder when playing a round of golf. This can lead to a higher shoulder on the side that you carry your bag on. This is because to compensate the body raises the shoulder on the side of where the golf bag strap is carried. This is so the golf bag won't come off the shoulder when walking and to sustain the weight. Years of wearing the golf bag on the shoulder can lead to faulty posture with a higher shoulder on one side of the body and muscular imbalance. Think about it, it would not seem beneficial to carry a 25 to 40 pound luggage on one's shoulder for 5 miles to an airport, which is about the total walking length of a golf course. If you prefer to walk during a round of golf, I recommend using a motorized pull cart. In this way, you can get the benefit of walking without logging around a heavy golf bag. If a motorized pull cart is too expensive, a regular pull cart is also better than carrying your clubs.

However, make sure to switch hands after each hole when you pull the cart. In this way, this can lessen the stress of pulling on the shoulder and wrist joints. This is why the best option is a motorized pull cart that you don't have to pull. It goes by itself usually by a remote. I still think the fastest way to play golf when there aren't many golfers on the course, is to use an electric golf cart. When practicing on the driving range, please be aware of the other golfers. Some driving ranges really put people too close to one another. Make sure to stand as far as possible away from another golfer. Sometimes a golfer can be hurt by an errant golf shot from another golfer swinging nearby. When a golfer hits a shank, it can be especially dangerous. Shanks are hit in an almost lateral direction. This can be especially dangerous at circular type driving ranges. Circular type driving ranges have the practicing golfers lined up in semi-circle arrangement at one end of the driving range. Just be conscious of who is hitting next to you at the driving range. Unfortunately, there can be a few golfers at the golf range that can be careless and don't think twice about putting someone in harm's way.

When lifting your golf bag from the ground, there is an easy procedure to follow. You first should bend at your knees and then lift using your legs. Also, make sure the golf bag is as close as possible to you when lifting it. If you lift the bag further away from you, it will make the bag feel heavier. This puts more stress on the joints and lower back. Then finally straighten up the legs after lifting the bag. Be careful not to bang the hard bottom of the golf bag into your shins when lifting. Also, when teeing up a ball or picking up the ball from inside the cup, you should make sure to first bend with both knees. Avoid just bending at the waist to do these actions. Just bending at the waist may cause injury to the lower back. The incorrect way is demonstrated in *Figure 10.3*. The correct way is shown in *Figure 10.4*.

Figure 10.3

Figure 10.4

Footnotes

1. *Mosby's Guide to Physical Examination* by Henry M. Seidal, et al. Missouri: Mosby, 1995

Chapter 11
Swing Thoughts

Golfers generally are known to think too much before hitting the golf ball. Having too many swing thoughts while in the stance is not beneficial. After learning and using all the essentials of the zero handicap golfer or better (see Chapter 2), one should have specific swing thoughts. First, the swing thought that one should have before hitting the ball is on the target. The swing thought that one should have after hitting the ball is to finish high with the shaft of the club pointed to the sky with the 6-iron, 7-iron, 8-iron, 9-iron, pitching wedge and sand wedge on full shots. The swing thought one should have after hitting the ball is to finish with the shaft of the club pointed to the sky and to the side with the driver, 3-wood, 4-wood, 5-wood, 3-iron, 4-iron and 5-iron.

Many golfers today have too many thoughts running in their head about golf instruction at once. When learning the essentials of the zero handicap golfer or better, incorporate them into your swing into steps. First, make sure you are using the proper interlocking grip. Then as you go into your stance make sure your feet are approximately shoulders width apart. Make sure the back shoulder is lower than the front shoulder. Now align yourself with the position of the ball. The golf ball is aligned with the inside of the forward foot. Once you practice this a few times now move into the swing. The forward arm is bent at 90 to 95 degrees at the top of the backswing. Now go back and practice these four essentials again one more time. According to essential #5 of the zero handicap or better golf swing, weight begins to shift from the back foot to the forward foot when beginning the start of the downswing to hit the ball. In golf, as well as in other sports, one must go back to go forward to maximize power. Tennis players and baseball hitters, who can hit the ball the hardest, have the most powerful weight shifts. Golf doesn't work any different. The more powerful your weight shift, the faster the ball will go. If a ball is hit hard enough at the right launch angle, the ball will go extremely far. It's pretty simple. Just like in baseball sometimes a ball can be hit very hard on a line, which is maybe only 10 feet off the ground. This ball might even be caught by the second baseman. This is called a line drive. However, if this same ball was hit with the same speed to 40 feet off the ground, it would be well over the fence for a home run. Same with golf, a ball can be hit very hard on the line say maybe only 10 feet high. However, to maximize distance, the ball must be hit higher. Depending on swing speeds, the optimal launch angles are between 11 and 15 degrees. Generally, the lower launch angles between 11 and 13 are for golfers with higher clubhead speeds. Generally, the high launch angles of 14 and 15 degrees are for golfers with medium to low clubhead speeds.

Now after the club hits the ball, according to essential #6, you start to finish the downswing with a straight, stiff forward leg. The stiff forward leg is evidence of a great weight shift. Then follow essentials #7 and #8, which require high follow-throughs. Review the whole swing again and keep practicing. Your golf shots should progressively get closer to your targets. Patience, self-discipline and devotion will also help one improve at a faster rate. These essentials of the zero handicap golfer or better are here to help you enjoy golf more and in the process show you what it takes to play your best golf. Having low expectations in golf will most likely guarantee low results. If your ultimate goal is just to break 90, then that is where you might stay. To reach goals, as I said before, is to take baby steps. First, break 90 then 85 and so on. However, always have in the back of your mind what you intend to accomplish later on. If you are an 18-handicap golfer now, don't ever think being a zero handicap golfer is out of the question. Give yourself high expectations. For example, when I was a 14-handicap back in my second year of playing, I never let go of high expectations for myself. I planned for myself that if I kept on practicing I could consistently shoot below 70 on any course. My high expectations helped me to reach my goals. Of course, there was sometimes doubt in my mind if I could reach them, especially, when I reached a point of consistently shooting in the low to mid-eighties. I think when I finally did break 80 with a score of 79; it was a breakthrough for me. The score of anything in the seventies sounded like a professional score. Once I did finally get a 79, it made me feel then I could break 75. Then after 75, it was the goal of consistently breaking 70 and so on and so on. The main idea is to keep your long-term goals high and your short-term goals in baby steps.

The doubt that I sometimes had in myself in my first few years of playing golf was probably from listening to golf commentary and my playing partners. Things I would here would be like "golf is such a hard game", or "how can anyone play better than professional golfers." The best one was "how can anyone be consistent at golf." In fact, some would even be so impressed and star-awed by professional golfers that in their mind they already counted themselves out for being capable of playing at that high level. These people have already limited themselves and counted themselves as not good enough. Remember professional athletes are humans also. They go to the bathroom just like the rest of us. Nobody is a god except God Himself of course. Start to give yourself the reverence that many professional golfers receive. Start seeing yourself as capable of getting birdies or even eagles. My point is to change your mindset if you have not already. I stopped listening to what others said about the game of golf because it was not helping me. When I started to see myself as a master golfer, I felt capable. I was now capable to achieve whatever I set my mind to. I took control now. I was not going to let other unhelpful opinions limit me. I was not going to be a 14-handicap golfer stuck at the same handicap level for 20 years. As I said before, the majority is often wrong. Dare to have high expectations. You might just get what you set as your goals.

Keeping the club on the ground before hitting the golf ball

Before hitting a golf shot some golfers prefer to waggle the club off the ground (**Figure 11.1**). I prefer to let the club stay on the ground before hitting a shot except for in hazards and sand traps where grounding the club is against the rules. I like to keep the club on the ground as I set up to the golf ball because this way it is easier to control the angle of the clubface (**Figure 11.2**). When you waggle the club above the ground, it can lead to inconsistency because the clubface could end up being in different positions when finally hitting the ball. These different positions can lead to uncontrolled slices, hooks and shots that are hit too high or too low. With keeping the club on the ground before hitting the shot, the clubface should stay in the proper position to hit consistent shots. In this way, yardage can be controlled and accuracy can only improve.

Keep the golf game as simple as possible. Avoid using more than one wedge for chips. The sand wedge should be used on all chip shots. Having more than one wedge for chipping makes chipping much harder. This is because now one is dealing with two different lofts and two different club lengths. If one needs to put a little more loft on a shot, just open the clubface on the sand wedge and hit off the toe of the clubface just like in other chip shots.

Figure 11.1. This is the incorrect way. Avoid wobbling the club before hitting the ball.

Figure 11.2. This is the correct way to position the driver which is on the ground.

Chapter 12

Tournament Play: How to Play Your Best

Whether playing in an amateur or professional tournament, never give up. I know this is harder said than done. However, what is great about a golf tournament is that one does not have to come in first to have a pretty good tournament. Coming in the top 25% of a tournament is also good. Even beating 50% of the players in the field is not bad either. Of course, winning feels better. I know the golf ego loves to win. However, the zero handicap or better golfer lets go of his golf ego to play better golf. Letting go of the golf ego will take pressure off your game and make you play the best possible golf you can. However, the nature of a golf tournament is based on ego. Think about it. Everyone is trying to beat the other person to prove that he or she is superior and number one. I am personally not crazy about competitions because they sometimes bring out the ugly side in people. Because most golfers are controlled by their golf ego, many will do almost anything to win. This includes name-calling, using subtle, sly remarks, accusing another golfer of cheating, yelling, general harassment, and provoking fights. This is done all in the intent to throw the other golfer's timing and focus off. Golfers who do this are usually quite insecure and ruled by their golf ego. If they let go of their golf ego, they wouldn't feel so threatened by others. When golfers are competing, it makes some feel quite stressed. There is one way to stop the stress of competing. Let go of that golf ego. Whether one comes in first or last, his or her self-worth is not attached. In other words, detach self-worth with what place you come in. In fact, play in a tournament with the intent of not impressing others or the fear of embarrassing yourself. This is accomplished once again by letting go of the golf ego. Nobody really cares if you do great or do poorly. Therefore, when in a golf tournament, mentally feel like you are playing by yourself. Other golfers in the tournament are really only caring about what they are scoring. Let the pressure go by letting go of that golf ego. You will find now that you will have more fun. Golf is a game and is meant to be played as such. Games are supposed to be fun. Why play a game if it is not fun? Even if you are playing in a professional tournament for money or your annual company tournament for a gift certificate to the pro shop, you should have fun. Money and prizes are one of the biggest pleasers to the golf ego. Once again, detach how much you win or first place with how good you are. In fact, doing this will make it easier to win because there will be less pressure and more fun. There is enough stress in some other parts of life. Why make golf also stressful and a pressure intense event? For example, the expression "put your game face on" is stupid. I know the intent was to get focused. I always perceived "put your game face on" as now it is time to get tense, anxious and nervous before your tournament. I would just get rid of this saying all together.

When playing in a tournament, one bad shot does not dictate your next shot. Every shot is an individual occurrence. Using the techniques of the zero handicap golfer or better should make each shot easier to make. If one happens to hit a bad shot, he should not take out his anger on the next shot. Sometimes people self-defeat themselves in crucial times in tournaments. Some golfers want to sabotage their success by hitting another poor shot almost on purpose because of their anger from the previous bad shot. Always play every shot with your best effort. You never know when the current first place golfer might fold up and start making bogeys. Don't give up because if you do, you will guarantee to lose. Avoid getting angry with yourself if a poor shot is hit. Always follow the shots. Avoid looking away if the ball goes in a place that you don't want it to. You can't rely on your playing partners to help you look for your ball. Have patience with yourself. The zero handicap golfer or better has patience with oneself. He or she knows that odds will eventually go in his or her favor. There is nothing like the satisfaction of accomplishing one's goals with practice and self-discipline.

Chapter 13
Golf Etiquette

The etiquette of golf doesn't make sense at times. Other sports like baseball really don't have much etiquette. For example, there is so much noise from the crowd in a baseball game whether it's people cheering or yelling at a player. However, in golf everyone must be quiet before a player hits a shot. If a golfer is really focused, the noise in the background should not be distracting. I think because golfers are brought up with this very traditional, etiquette when beginning to play. Also, when putting, other golfers should not move. This is ridiculous also. In other sports, there is constant movement. If you can play good golf without being distracted by sudden movements or sounds, you will be able to do your best in a golf tournament. Many golfers have played other sports, like baseball and basketball where there are always sounds and noise in the background. Look at golf in the same way. Avoid making one of your playing partners distract you by he or she talking in the background when your about to hit a shot. Remember it takes much more concentration to hit a baseball than hitting a golf ball. This is because in baseball you are dealing with a ball that is moving and trying to figure out in a half a second or less if it is a strike or ball. Also, think when you are on the golf range. Some golf ranges are filled with lots of people making noise and laughing in the background. Yet, most of us are not distracted by this. How about when we practice chipping and putting on the practice green with other golfers using the same green. Here we are usually not distracted either. Bring this concentration out to the golf course when you play a round.

In golf, everyone must be quiet and not say a word. It doesn't make much sense. I think professional golfers would not be distracted by clicking cameras and people talking if people were permitted to act as they do at a baseball game or basketball game. This is to talk and make noise when the golfer is hitting a shot. However, when playing, adhere to good, golf etiquette. Be considerate of your playing partners and be quiet when they are hitting a shot and don't make sudden movements. Since we are playing golf, there are etiquette rules that we must abide by especially when you're playing with strangers or potential business clients. Unfortunately, many golfers might perceive someone with bad golf etiquette as someone they would not like to associate with.

Chapter 14
Helpful Hints for Eating Right That Can Benefit Your Game

One thing that definitely slows people down as far as energy is eating red meat. Red meat takes longer to digest and takes more energy from the body than other foods such as whole-wheat pasta and vegetables. Red meat, as we know, is not good for the heart since it can lead to high triglycerides (high fat content) in the blood. This can lead to the clogging of arteries and heart disease. The number one cause of death in the U.S. has been heart disease. The second is cancer. Eating red meat has been linked with heart disease and cancer. If one is concerned about getting enough protein, other high sources exist such as wheat gluten and soy protein. Many veggie burgers, veggie hot dogs and veggie chicken patties are made with soy protein isolate. Veggie burgers today do taste like meat. Morning Star Farms® make a product called Better 'n Burgers,® which are delicious veggie burgers that taste like real hamburgers.[1] However, they are very healthy and have lots of protein. These are not the veggie burgers of years ago. The ones from years ago have less protein and were not very filling. Today the veggie burgers have evolved into food that is very tasty, filling and with lots of protein. The brand LightLife® makes chicken patties that are excellent, too. My 10-year-old niece couldn't tell the difference between these veggie-chicken patties and real chicken patties. This says a lot because children usually have more sensitive taste buds than that of adults. There are so many ways to prepare these chicken patties. Veggie-chicken parmesan is one option, and the typical lettuce tomato and mayo on a bun is another. LightLife® also makes a product called Smart Bacon.® It's not real bacon it is veggie bacon with the same texture of beacon without all that animal fat and grease. I make BLT's with Smart Bacon® and they taste very good in the morning.[2] Eating vegetarian can give one more energy, which is essential on the golf course.

The day before a round of golf, I would eat whole-wheat pasta with my own freshly made marinara sauce and a veggie-meatball parmesan hero (called hoagie in Philadelphia). Like a marathon runner, a golfer also needs a lot of energy on the golf course to think logically, clearly and have stores of physical energy. Here is my recipe for marinara sauce. Pour about two ounces of olive oil in a source pan. Mince five cloves of fresh garlic on the side. Put the five minced cloves of garlic in the saucepan. Saute the garlic in the olive oil for about 3-4 minutes on medium flame. However, do this until you only see a couple of little pieces of garlic turn slightly tan. Be careful not to wait too long, otherwise, it will burn. Then put one can of crushed tomatoes (28 ounces) in the saucepan and about three ounces of tomato paste to thicken the sauce. Add salt, oregano, quarter cup of onions and a teaspoon of organic brown sugar. Stir the sauce 200 times. Then after stirring put a cover on the sauce pan for 30 minutes and let it cook on a low flame. Trader Joe's® makes a great veggie meatball that you can use to make meatball parmesan.[3]

Staying away from red meat will also save cattle in our environment. Over 375 million cattle have been killed in this country due to meat consumption since 1990. Whether one agrees or not with saving animals, eating vegetarian will increase one's chances of living longer and having a better quality of life. Eating meat can produce free radicals, which can result in premature aging. There are some myths about eating vegetarian, too. It is not true that eating vegetarian will make one lose muscle. In fact, since I started being a vegetarian, I began to gain muscle, which made me gain 20 pounds over a three year span. I have a good weight-lifting program that I follow along with a vegetarian diet that has let to more muscle and less fat on my body. This will be explained in the next chapter. For example, a gorilla, which is a vegetarian, has the strength of 10 men and is big and strong with lots of muscles. One doesn't need meat to be strong or have big muscles. I don't eat red meat, chicken or dairy. I do eat soy cheese, which is a great dairy substitute. The soy cheese nowadays is so like regular cheese that one can't tell the difference. I use mozzarella soy cheese on my veggie chicken hero and veggie meatball hero. I do eat lettuce, broccoli, spinach, various fruits and some health bars. I have found eating this way has helped me maintain my consistency in golf. My mind is much clearer and I have even more power than before. There are some vegetarians that are very skinny because they are not getting enough plant-based protein in their meals. This is why some vegetarians appear to be so thin. Before I was a vegetarian, I used to eat lots of hamburgers and steaks. The hamburgers used to make me feel so bloated. The steaks used to make me fall asleep. In fact, as a teenager I used to think that this was normal to fall asleep after eating steak. It was the high saturated fat content that made me fall asleep and the added energy it took my body to digest it. I also drink lots of water now, which is very important.

When I play golf, I make sure to bring a soy cheese sandwich on whole wheat bread. After about nine holes, I eat and this gives me some energy. I also bring organic pretzels. It helps to replenish my salt content.

Vitamins

Vitamin A is important for normal vision, defense against bacteria, healthy skin, and bone development. It is an antioxidant. Antioxidants fight against free-radicals, which can cause changes to the normal DNA in the body. Free radicals can cause cancer. Deficiency of vitamin A can cause night blindness. Having adequate intake of vitamin A can help one see better when reading putts in the early morning or late afternoon to early evening when there are more shadows to contend with. The shadows sometimes make the greens look darker in certain spots. However, excessive intake of vitamin A can cause temporary baldness and joint pain.

Food Sources of Vitamin A

fish liver oils	cantaloupe	kale	mango
egg yolks	spinach	carrots	sweet potatoes
cheese	broccoli	sweet peppers	apricots

Vitamin B1 or thiamine helps the heart and nerves function properly. It is essential because it aids in the release of energy from fats, proteins and carbohydrates. Carbohydrates are used by the body in endurance events for energy such as playing a round of golf.

Food Sources of Vitamin B1

whole grain bread	sunflower seeds	whole grain cereal

dry beans	acorn squash	peas
peanuts	potatoes	lentils

Vitamin B2 or riboflavin also aids in the release of energy from fats, proteins and carbohydrates. Deficiency of this vitamin can cause glossitis, which is inflammation of the tongue. Also, deficiency can cause red, flaky skin and cheilosis, which is cracking at the corners of the mouth. Most importantly, deficiencies can also cause general fatigue.

Food Sources of Vitamin B2

eggs	whole grain cereal	asparagus
soymilk	whole grain bread	broccoli
milk	banana	soy cheese

Vitamin B3 or niacin helps in the release of energy from fats, proteins and carbohydrates. Deficiencies can cause general fatigue and red, flaky skin. B-vitamins are important for maintaining energy through out the round of golf and in practice sessions.

Food Sources of Vitamin B3

peanut butter	whole grain bread	soymilk
yeast	whole grain cereal	asparagus
beans	milk	

Vitamin B5 or pantothenic aids in the metabolism of fats and carbohydrates. Deficiency can cause nerve transmission problems. Nerve transmission is what causes muscles to move. Pantothenic acid is important for good, healthy nerves so coordination won't be impaired.

Food Sources of Vitamin B5

avocados	milk	soybeans
broccoli	lentils	cashew nuts
eggs	peanuts	whole grain cereals

Vitamin B6 or pyridoxine is needed for healthy skin and proper nerve function. Deficiencies may cause skin disorders and anemia. Anemia will make one tired because there is less oxygen in the blood. Once again, pyridoxine is needed to maintain energy levels in golf.

Food Sources of Vitamin B6

potatoes	spinach	garbanzo beans	soybeans
bananas	whole grain cereals	hummus	lima beans
watermelon	broccoli	sunflower seeds	soy cheese

Biotin is an important type of B vitamin for carbohydrate and fatty acid metabolism. So if one lacks biotin, energy levels can be decreased. Biotin deficiency can lead to red, scaly skin.

Food Sources of Biotin

soybeans	cauliflower	peanut butter
egg yolk	nuts	whole grain cereals
cheese	oatmeal	whole grain breads

Vitamin B9 or folic acid is needed for proper red blood cell function. It also helps to make DNA in our bodies. Deficiency of folic acid in pregnant women can cause abnormal brain and spinal cord development in the fetus. Folic acid deficiency can also lead to anemia, depression and confusion. Plenty of folic acid is required by golfers to help maintain endurance levels.

Food Sources of Vitamin B9

Green leafy vegetables	spinach	asparagus
beans	vegetarian baked beans	green peas
orange juice	avocado	wheat germ

Vitamin B12 or cobalamin is required for proper nerve function and in the making of DNA in the body. Deficiencies can cause poor vision, lack of coordination, poor balance and numbness in the legs and arms. Deficiencies can also cause anemia. If this type of anemia is not treated, it can be fatal. Balance and coordination are very important in golf. Balance is what we need so we can hit the ball on the center of the club and coordination lets us hit the ball where we aim at.

Food Sources of Vitamin B12

| eggs | milk | some brands of soymilk |

Vitamin C or ascorbic acid is needed for proper bone and connective tissue growth; it helps form collagen. Collagen is needed to maintain good, healthy skin. It also helps maintain the ligaments in our body. Vitamin C helps wounds to heal. In addition, it aids in proper blood vessel function and in the absorption of vitamin A and iron. Vitamin C is an antioxidant. It helps to protect the skin from sun damage. However, sunblock is always required when going outside in the daylight even when it is cloudy. Eating foods with vitamin C before and after playing golf outside is an added benefit in protecting us against the harmful rays of the sun. Please avoid making the mistake of only having foods with vitamin C and not wearing sunblock when playing golf. As I said before, sunblock is an absolute necessity when playing golf. Deficiency of vitamin C can cause scurvy. Symptoms of scurvy involve inflamed, bleeding gums, loss in density of bones and poor wound healing.

Food Sources of Vitamin C

oranges	cabbage	broccoli	cauliflower
strawberries	potatoes	cantaloupe	carrots
tomatoes	grapefruits	orange juice	sweet red pepper

Vitamin D is formed with sun exposure and in certain foods we eat. This vitamin is needed for proper absorption of calcium by the small intestine so bones can be strong. A deficiency of vitamin D can cause softening of bones, muscle spasm and abnormal bone growth. Vitamin D is needed for proper and consistent muscle contraction in golf. A form of vitamin D is also formed from sunlight in the skin.

Food Sources of Vitamin D

egg yolk	fish liver oil	soymilk	fortified cereal

Vitamin E is an antioxidant. It fights against free radicals in the body that can damage DNA. A deficiency of vitamin E can cause red blood cell damage and destruction to the nerves. Adequate amounts of vitamin E are needed for proper nerve function in the body, which greatly contributes to coordination in golf. Nerve impulses move muscle.

Food Sources of Vitamin E

green leafy vegetables	eggs	whole wheat bread
beans	whole grain cereal	nuts
vegetable oil		

Vitamin K is needed for blood to clot. For example, if one cuts oneself accidentally and the body has no vitamin K, the cut will keep bleeding. Vitamin K is also made by normal bacteria living in the small intestine. However, food sources are also needed to sustain proper levels of this vitamin.

Food Sources of Vitamin K

spinach	broccoli	cauliflower
cabbage	vegetable oil	kale
parsley	turnip greens	watercress

Protein

Protein is needed by the body to maintain and build muscle. Other functions of protein involve maintaining healthy skin, hair, nails, connective tissue and other cells of the body. However, most energy that we need when playing golf comes from the carbohydrates we eat.

Food Sources of Protein

soybeans	seitan	semolina pasta
veggie dog	tempeh	pinto beans
veggie burger	tofu	soymilk
lentils	black beans	whole wheat bread
almond butter	chickpeas	whole wheat pasta
soy yogurt	peanut butter	Bulgar wheat pancakes
veggie bologna	veggie turkey	veggie sausage
soy cheese	soy cheese	soy cheese
(American style)	(provolone style)	(mozzarella style)

Minerals

<u>Sodium</u> is needed for proper nerve and muscle function. Deficiency of sodium can lead to weakness and fatigue. In extreme deficiencies, it can lead to coma. Sodium comes from the salt that is added to food in our diets. Enough sodium is needed in the body when playing golf to avoid fatigue and confusion when setting up to hit a shot.

Food Sources of Sodium

soy cheese	potato chips	cornbread
sauerkraut	pizza	marinara sauce
olives	whole wheat bread	whole wheat pasta

<u>Potassium</u> is also needed for proper nerve and muscle function. Potassium is needed to maintain proper muscle contraction in golf. Sodium, chloride

and potassium are important minerals that are also in the form of electrolyte ions inside the body. They should remain at adequate levels during playing golf. If they go below adequate levels, muscle contraction and nerve conduction will be impaired leading to poor performance, fatigue and confusion.

Food Sources of Potassium

bananas	orange juice	peaches
prunes	broccoli	asparagus
raisins	spinach	lettuce

Calcium is important for maintaining bone and teeth. It plays a big part in the start of a muscle contraction. Calcium is important for healthy, strong muscular contractions. Low calcium levels in the body can lead to muscle spasm and a loss of bone density and bone mass in older adults. Excess levels of calcium can cause kidney failure. Calcium is important in golf to generate muscle contractions consistently.

Food Sources of Calcium

beans	soy cheese	almonds
broccoli	pizza	soymilk
tofu	turnip greens	green beans
tempeh	tahini	kale

Phosphorus is a mineral that is needed for formation of DNA in all the cells of the body. It is involved with muscle contraction and nerves. Phosphorus is needed to have good muscle contraction in golf. Deficiencies of phosphorus can cause weakness and poor bone formation.

Food Sources of Phosphorus

almonds	eggs	green peas
tofu	peanut butter	whole wheat bread

Iron is a main structure of muscle cells and red blood cells. A deficiency of iron will cause weakness and anemia. Adequate levels of iron maintain our energy levels in golf, make us think clearer and help in bringing oxygen to all the cells of the body.

Food Sources of Iron

soybeans	chickpeas	lima beans	peaches
lentils	veggie burger	black beans	tahini
tofu	tempeh	spinach	black-eyed peas
kidney beans	pinto beans	turnip greens	prunes

Zinc is needed for certain hormones in the body. It is also plays a role in immunity, maintaining healthy skin and in the healing of wounds. Zinc is also important in helping us see when it is darker outside like on cloudy days and when we play golf in the early morning.

Food Sources of Zinc

lima beans	soy	nuts
eggs	peanut butter	whole wheat bread

Copper helps in the making of red blood cells in the body and in the synthesis of new bone. A deficiency of copper can cause anemia, which will cause fatigue and weakness. Deficiencies of copper can cause loss of energy for golf and reduced concentration. Inadequate intake of copper has also been linked with premature graying of hair. However, excess amounts of copper can cause copper deposits in the brain and cornea and liver damage, which can be very serious.

Food Sources of Copper

eggs	spinach	peas
whole wheat bread	beets	nuts
asparagus	beans	whole grain cereal

Manganese plays a role in breaking down carbohydrates and in regulating blood sugar levels.

Food Sources of Manganese

nuts	non-leafy vegetables	whole grain cereal
whole grain bread	dried fruits	tea
beans	green leaf vegetables	fresh fruits

Selenium is a mineral and also considered an antioxidant, which fights against free radicals in the body that are associated with aging and cancer.

Food Sources of Selenium

Brazil nuts	garlic	whole wheat pasta
whole wheat bread	mushrooms	egg yolk

Chromium helps in the metabolism of carbohydrates and fats. Chromium helps to maintain normal blood sugar levels.

Food Sources of Chromium

nuts	whole wheat bread	whole grain cereal
wheat germ	brewer's yeast	

Iodine is needed by the thyroid gland to make thyroid hormones. These hormones help to control the rate of the body's metabolism. Deficiency of iodine can cause hypothyroidism, which can cause one's metabolism to decrease leading to weight gain and sluggishness. Iodine is needed to maintain metabolism at normal levels so one can have adequate energy to play long rounds of golf.

Food Sources of Iodine

iodized salt

vegetables that are grown in iodine rich soil

Magnesium is required to maintain normal muscle and nerve function. Low levels of magnesium can lead to impaired nerves leading to decreased coordination in golf.

Food Sources of Magnesium

spinach	lettuce	kidney beans
lima beans	peanut butter	chick peas
broccoli	tomato	potatoes

Footnotes

1. Morningstar Farms and Better 'n Burgers are registered trademarks of Kellogg Company, which was not involved in the production of, and does not endorse, this product.

2. Lightlife and Smart Bacon are registered trademarks of Lightlife Foods, Inc., which was not involved in the production of, and does not endorse, this product.

3. Trader Joe's is a registered trademark of Trader Joe's Inc., which was not involved in the production of, and does not endorse this product.

Water Consumption in Golf

I bring a lot of water with me when I play golf. I usually bring about one gallon in the summer and spring and about 64 ounces in the winter and fall months. I have a distiller at home that makes distilled water. Distilled water is the best water to drink. This is because there is nothing but water in this; it is 100% water. Distilled water can also be bought in the bottled water form. However, it must say distilled for it to be distilled. If it says something like, spring water or filtered water, it is not distilled. Also, check the date on the bottled water. If the date is too old, plastic can leak into the water and can contaminate it. Water from the faucet usually is already contaminated with chlorine. Chlorine is used as a disinfectant against bacteria and other microbes. However, ingestion of chlorine by drinking or inhalation can cause serious side effects. Some side effects may include skin redness and flaking. There are many other hazardous substances in water from the faucet that can lead to health problems. It is very important to watch what you drink. Taking a shower also may be somewhat hazardous. Since there is chlorine in our water supply, it is important to use a water filter in the shower also that filters out chlorine water. While taking a shower, chlorine vapors can be hazardous to health. Taking a shower with water that contains chlorine can cause skin rashes. Pure water is needed for our bodies as a source of purifying our own bodies. The kidneys need plenty of water to filter out things that can harm our body. In addition, our blood is 98% water. Without enough water, one can dehydrate. Our bodies are 75% water. Therefore, it makes a lot of sense to be properly hydrated.

When not exercising or playing golf, one should drink about half the amount of his or her weight measured in ounces. All the organs in the body need water for survival and for optimum health. For example, a 200-pound male should drink 100 ounces of water per day. Another example is that a 142-pound female should drink about 71 ounces per day. However, on days with exercise and playing golf, water intake should be increased. A good way to tell if you are properly hydrated is to check the color of your urine. If the urine is clear in color, this usually means that one is properly hydrated. If the urine is a very deep yellow, this usually means that one needs to drink more water.

As some people get older, they may lose an inch or so in height. Some contribute this to the process of aging. However, the reason so many people lose height is because of not maintaining adequate water levels in the body. Some people don't drink enough water and over time leads to thinning of the discs in the spine. There are discs between each vertebra in the back. These discs serve as shock absorption when we walk, jog, sit or stand. These discs are mostly made of water. When we are not properly hydrated over time, these discs will lose water. This leads to thinning of discs, which causes people to lose height. The thinning of discs can lead to a form of arthritis in the spine called osteoarthritis. This can cause a decreased range of motion in the spine, which is not a good thing for playing golf. A decreased range of motion may lead to less control of the golf swing. This can cause inconsistency in golf. Because one gets older is not a reason why we must lose height and range of motion in the spine. In my opinion, one significant reason is a deficiency of water intake. The loss of height is due to a deficiency of water intake over many years. Also, working out the muscles is something that should be continued to keep the muscles and bones strong. Thus, strength is maintained and increased even as we get older. Approximately 40% of a person's height is made up of the spine. The vertebral column (spine) is composed of bones called vertebrae, which serve to protect the spinal cord from injury. The vertebrae can help in flexing, rotating and extending the spine. Notice these are the movements in the golf swing. Muscles of the back are attached to these vertebrae. There are 26 vertebrae in the normal adult. There are seven cervical vertebrae. Cervical vertebrae start at the bottom of the back of the head to the top of the back. Cervical vertebrae are smaller than other vertebrae of the spine. The first cervical vertebra is called C1, which starts at the bottom of the back of the head. The second cervical vertebra is called C2 and is right below C1. Between each vertebra in the spine, except between C1 and C2, are discs as discussed before. These discs act as shock absorbers so when one walks or plays golf the vertebrae don't jam into one another. There are 12 thoracic vertebrae in the spine. Thoracic means pertaining to the chest. Below the 12 thoracic vertebrae are 5 lumbar vertebrae in the spine. Below the lumbar vertebrae are fused portions called the sacrum and finally the coccyx, which is our tailbone. It is important to have strong muscles in the back because they move the bones in our spine. If the muscles in the back are not strong, the spine will move ineffectively when striking the golf ball. In this way, inconsistency can result leading to high scores and a slow rate of improvement. Our muscles need to be strong to gain greater clubhead speed and control of the golf club when swinging.

Chapter 15

The Workout for Added Strength and Endurance in Golf

I do have a workout, which I maintain to keep me strong and to gain strength. It is a combination of cardiovascular exercise such as jogging, walking, elliptical machine and weightlifting. I do work out at my local health club. I definitely advise joining one. It doesn't have to be that expensive either. There are many health clubs that have the needed equipment at a reasonable price. My strength training workout consists of doing various weight machines. In fact, I concentrate on working out both upper and lower bodies in every exercise session. Added strength will let you hit the ball further because of increased clubhead speed. I perform strength training exercises three times a week. It takes approximately 75 to 120 minutes to complete in each session depending on how many machines I do. I'm going to break down the weightlifting exercises in this one session between lower body and upper body. I work out my upper body and the lower body because they must both be strong. This way there is muscle balance in the body, and injury can be reduced. Most importantly, the weight shift will flow more easily, which will transfer power much more effectively into the golf ball. Weightlifting also strengthens bones and makes them more resistance to physical stress. This is important as we age. We don't have to lose muscle just because we get older. The way to keep muscles and our bones strong is by strength training. We can maintain our strength and even get stronger as we workout. Be advised that after working out, the muscles might be somewhat stiff for the first week or two.

However, this soreness will go away once you stick to your strength training on a consistent basis. As with any workout, please consult with your licensed health professional before performing.

Strength Training Exercises in the Lower Body to Increase Clubhead Speed in Golf

The muscles of the lower body are important for generating the speed of the weight shift. They are important for clubhead speed. They are responsible for first creating the initial power of the swing. Here is a list of strength training exercises for the lower body that I perform at the gym.

1. Seated Leg Press

2. Hip Abduction

3. Hip Adduction

4. Seated Leg Curl

5. Leg Extension

6. Squats

7. Standing Calf Raise

8. Seated Calf Raise

9. Seated Shin Exercise

10. Standing Shin Exercise

Strength Training Exercises in the Upper Body to Increase Clubhead Speed in Golf

The muscles in the upper body also are quite important in the generation of clubhead speed. The power force from the legs is transferred to the muscles of the upper body. In this way, if the upper body is strong like the lower body, the transfer of this power force is highly effective and clubhead speed will be increased. Thus, the muscles of the body will be in balance helping in the prevention of injury and maximizing one's power. Here is a list of strength training exercises for the upper body that I perform at the gym.

1. Seated Row Machine

2. Incline Chest Press

3. Butterfly

4. Biceps Curls

5. Forearm Curl

6. Reverse Forearm Curl with dumbbell

7. Shoulder Press

8. Bar Dips

9. Cable Push-Down

10. Lat Pulls

11. Lumbar Extension

(Low Back Extension)

12. Regular Chest Press

13. Abdominal Crunch

14. Lateral Raise

Aerobic Exercises to Gain Endurance in Golf

It is always good to warm up before strength training. Walking a mile on the treadmill or doing the elliptical machine for a mile is excellent for getting your muscles warm and ready for strength training. On the days off from strength training, I recommend doing these aerobic exercises. I usually do about 12 miles of a combination of jogging on the treadmill, elliptical machine and walking in a week. It is beneficial to do a combination of cardiovascular exercise because it puts less stress on the joints of the body. Sometimes if one just jogs for aerobic exercise and nothing else, this could lead to knee and ankle pain down the road. I do these three aerobic exercises as a way of maintaining my energy in a round of golf. Make sure to always have good running sneakers to jog in. This is essential. Avoid wearing worn out sneakers. This can lead to injury to the knee and ankle joints. Wearing the proper sneakers may prevent joint pain in the future. In addition, if you do choose to jog, make sure to jog on a track or on a treadmill. This is because a track or treadmill reduces the stress on your ankle joints and lower back. If you only have access to jogging on concrete, make sure you don't jog on a surface that is sloped to the left or to the right. This also can prevent injury down the road.

Chapter 16
Golf Progression

After learning and applying these techniques in this book, your score should continue to improve. However, it is important to create a file for yourself of your golf statistics after every round. I also highly recommend counting the number of golf shots you take every week. Golf shots to count include putts, chips, fairway wood shots, drives and iron shots. In this way, you can monitor your golf improvement. Here is a list of statistics that you should keep. Name of course, regular course rating, course rating of golf course factoring in the effect of wind (see chapter 7), your score, the date, average temperature, putts per round, scrambling percentage, greens in regulation percentage, driving accuracy percentage, average driving distance for two drives in each round. Keeping these statistics will show your improvement and give you motivation to stick to your goals. This file is also a great place to list your goals. For example, a goal can be written like this. _____(Your Name) is a zero handicap golfer by June 12, 20__ (fill in the date.) One of the most important golf statistics is greens hit in regulation. This is the percentage of times a ball is hit on the green in two or more shots below par. This statistic correlates greatly with how low one can score.

May you reach your goals with ease in golf, and always believe in yourself. I thank you for giving me this opportunity to share with you the key techniques for becoming a zero handicap golfer or better.